D1709084

Charles Bridges
and
William Dering

FRONTISPIECE. *Mann Page II*, by Charles Bridges.

Charles Bridges

and

William Dering

Two Virginia Painters,

1735 - 1750

By

GRAHAM HOOD

Published by
THE COLONIAL WILLIAMSBURG FOUNDATION
Williamsburg, Virginia

Distributed by
THE UNIVERSITY PRESS OF VIRGINIA
Charlottesville, Virginia

Printed in the United States of America

Library of Congress Cataloging in Publication Data

Hood, Graham, 1936–
    Charles Bridges and William Dering.

    1. Bridges, Charles, 1670–1747.   2. Dering,
William.   3. Portraits—Virginia—Catalogs.
I. Title.
ND1329.B75H66   759.155   77–13772
ISBN 0–87935–047–4

For my Son

Jorin

Table of Contents

List of Illustrations

ix

Preface

CHARLES BRIDGES has been a mystifying figure to students of American painting, hovering at the edge of our consciousness in a penumbra of few facts and many misattributed portraits. His work in Virginia has been neglected by virtually every historian in favor of the better documented career of John Smibert, who arrived in America only six years earlier than Bridges and who chose the smaller and less affluent colony of Massachusetts in which to practice his art. It will be seen that Bridges's portraits have much in common—both in terms of quality and stylistic origin—with those of Smibert, which have been widely regarded as the fountainhead of American eighteenth-century painting.

It fell, in New England and Pennsylvania, to the eminently capable Robert Feke to build on the solid achievement of Smibert. In Virginia the comparable achievement of Bridges devolved upon the frail, if rather engaging, talent of William Dering. Characterized by a freshness that verges on naiveté but a restricted technique, the better of Dering's portraits make up in imaginative fancy for what they lack in power.

Twenty-five years ago Bridges was the subject of intensive research by Henry Wilder Foote, whose long article in the *Virginia Magazine of History and Biography* was the first attempt to define the artist and his work in a systematic manner. Dr. Foote's professed bias, however, was toward history and genealogy rather than the paintings themselves, with the result that the group of portraits he attributed to Bridges has never appeared cohesive or consistent. Thomas E. Thorne pondered the question of these attributions for some years; his article in *Arts in Virginia* in 1969 dealt directly with the core of the problem. This excellent approach, combined with Professor Thorne's characteristically shrewd observations, kindly imparted to me at the beginning of my work on Bridges, helped enormously, and I am very grateful to him. I have also benefited by the permission of Susanne Neale Fox to quote from her unpublished M.A. thesis dealing with the known facts of Bridges's life in England, which gives us a much clearer picture of what kind of man this was who left us some powerful and memorable images of early Virginia gentry.

In the issue of the *Virginia Magazine* that contained Foote's article on Bridges also appeared the first systematic study of William Dering, by the noted authority on southern arts, J. Hall Pleasants. Little documentary information can be added to what is recounted there; indeed, only in the last few years has any serious attempt been made to attribute more portraits to this artist. Carolyn J. Weekley published an excellent note in the first issue of *Journal of Early Southern Decorative Arts* (1975), persuasively adding two attractive pictures to the list of Dering's works. To Miss Weekley I am grateful for sharing her knowledge of the subject, and I acknowledge with pleasure Frank L. Horton's making available the research files of the Museum of Early Southern Decorative Arts in Winston-Salem, North Carolina.

My interest in these two artists has been much sustained by the enthusiasm of my wife, of Margaret Gill, and of Molly Prince. Gale Hood asked the right skeptical questions as she witnessed a group of photographs of early Virginia portraits make an arduous transition —during the slow and often capricious accumulation of information and insights—from a file marked "Scowling Phizzog. Limner" to one finally marked "Charles Bridges." Mrs. Gill checked countless historical details and made acute observations of her own; without her diligence this study would not have been completed. Miss Prince assisted materially during her year as museum intern in the Department of Collections at Colonial Williamsburg, contributing as least as much as she gained.

Dr. and Mrs. Thomas A. Graves, Jr., have allowed me to disrupt their household several times to study the important paintings owned by the College of William and Mary that adorn the President's House there. I am deeply grateful for their enthusiastic cooperation. John M. Jennings most kindly gave me useful information and pointed me in exactly the right direction several times. Louise L. Kale and Henry D. Grunder have been generous with their time and energies, and Robert G. Stewart, Monroe H. Fabian, and Ellen G. Miles have been kind colleagues.

As the portraits of these artists present no consistent chronology, I have not attempted to interweave a discussion of them into a recounting of the biographical documentation of the two men. Rather I have fallen back on the old-fashioned approach of treating the lives and the works separately; in this way I believe a clearer discussion of the hitherto unattributed pictures is offered.

In a number of cases the owners of portraits that I have attributed to Charles Bridges have believed that the people portrayed were of a different and earlier generation than the painter could possibly have known. Certain owners have inherited portraits discussed here that have traditionally been thought to represent members of their family who were dead even before the seventeenth century was out. Since my concern has been primarily with the identity of the artist rather than of the sitters, I have not attempted to ascribe a new identity to the subjects portrayed in most cases, but have instead used generalized titles, which are indicated by quotation marks. When a name suggested for the subject seems to me to be a reasonable one, I have used italics. These, of course, are my own opinions.

FIGURE 4. *Mrs. Mann Page II and child*, by Charles Bridges.

FIGURE 22. "Girl of the Ludwell family," by Charles Bridges.

Charles Bridges

C HARLES BRIDGES was the fourth son of John and Elizabeth Trumbull Bridges and was christened at Barton Seagrave, Northamptonshire, on April 2, 1670. His family were gentry and at least two of his brothers achieved some modest distinction, John, an antiquarian whose voluminous writings were published posthumously as *The History and Antiquities of Northamptonshire*, and William, who became secretary of the government Stamp Office in London. Charles Bridges married Alice Flower on August 4, 1687, at St. Marylebone's, near London. In 1699 he became active as an agent for the Society for Promoting Christian Knowledge. Founded in that year, the society addressed itself to missionary work and making available Christian literature, as well as to the terrible plight of the poor in England. By developing an organized system of charity schools and workhouses, the society strove to supplement the efforts that had been made continuously by the government since Elizabethan times to tackle one of England's most persistent and insidious problems. As an agent, Bridges maintained close contacts with the locally developed charity schools—by 1705, there were over fifty of them in London—and channeled advice, moral support, and occasionally financial assistance from the society to the local trustees.[1]

---

[1] Most of the information pertaining to Bridges's English career is derived from Susanne Neale, "Charles Bridges: Painter and Humanitarian" (M.A. thesis, College of William and Mary, 1969), copy, Research Library, Colonial Williamsburg Foundation. See also W. O. B. Allen and Edmund McClure, *Two Hundred Years: The History of The Society for Promoting Christian Knowledge, 1698–1898* (London, 1898), and W. K. Lowther Clarke, *A History of the S.P.C.K.* (London, 1959). If Bridges was, as stated, 77 at the time of his death, he must have been born in 1670.

Until 1713 Bridges's name appeared frequently in the records of the Society for Promoting Christian Knowledge. His special concern was with the schools, mainly in London but also dotted throughout the country, that sought to offer some glimmer of hope to the most desperately oppressed members of the society of that time—deprived children. His involvement with the society gives us a measure of his character.

From 1713 until 1733 there is no mention of Bridges in the society's records. Presumably he pursued another career; if it was an artistic one, he appears to have gained little distinction. Of this period of Bridges's life only two facts, at present, are known. First, he painted a portrait of the Reverend Thomas Baker, fellow of St. John's College, Cambridge, after 1717 when Baker was ejected from his fellowship. Five painted versions of this portrait exist, none of them signed or dated; an engraving by John Simon fortunately gives information about the artist and sitter. Second, Bridges was in touch with Richard Roach, fellow of St. John's College, Oxford, at some time before the latter's death in 1730 concerning illustrations for a book (a hymnal?) probably written or edited by Roach.

How Bridges acquired his training is unknown; his name is not recorded in connection with Sir Godfrey Kneller. If he did not study with the principal portrait painter of the time, or at the Kneller Academy, it is possible that he was associated with Charles Jervas, whose reputation by 1723 was such that he succeeded Kneller as portrait painter to the king. Bridges's later portraits of Virginians give strong evidence of artistic kinship with one of these two dominant portrait painters of the period.[2]

---

[2] Henry Wilder Foote, "Charles Bridges: 'Sergeant-Painter of Virginia,' 1735-1740," *Virginia Magazine of History and Biography*, LX (January 1952), pp. 3-55, gives most of the relevant information about the Baker portraits (pp. 17-18), although he misquoted the inscription on the engraving—by omitting "Late" before "Fellow of St. John's Colledge" he allowed an erroneous date to be assigned to it and to the portraits. See also Thomas Thorne, "Charles Bridges, Limner," *Arts in Virginia*, IX (winter 1969), pp. 22-31, and p. 11 of this study. Bridges's undated letter to Roach is in the Rawlinson

In 1733, when he was in his sixties, Bridges wrote Henry Newman, secretary of the Society for Promoting Christian Knowledge,
that there was a "strong inclination in himself to go to Georgia and
should soon come to a Resolution ..." What prompted this "inclination" at such an advanced age is unknown—perhaps it was the neces-
sity to support a large family by his second marriage.[3] One might
have thought that his numerous and influential contacts would have
been of more benefit to him, unless he was by nature a restless spirit.
In any event, by May 1735 Bridges had arrived in Williamsburg,
accompanied by "daughters and son," and armed with letters of recommendation to the two most important men in the colony, Commissary James Blair and Lieutenant Governor William Gooch. On
May 26, 1735, Gooch wrote his brother, Thomas, master of Caius
College, Cambridge, and a canon of Canterbury, that he had received
Thomas's letter recommending Bridges "in a particular manner to
my esteem and favour." Gooch continued, "Mr. Bridges I have already loaded with my civilities, tho' it looks a little odd for a Gover-
nour to show so much favour to a Painter, as to lend him Coach to
fetch his Daughters and Son, and his waggon for two days to bring
up his Goods, and to entertain him at Dinner and Supper several
times since his arrival, and to promise him as soon as he's settled that
he shall begin to show the country his Art, by drawing my Picture,
but all this I have done, and upon yr. recommendation shall continue
to do him all the Service in my power."[4]

James Blair, the powerful deputy of the Bishop of London in Virginia and president of the College of William and Mary, wrote to
the Bishop on July 7, 1735: "I had your Lordship's lately by Mr.

Papers, Bodleian Library, Oxford, copy, Virginia Colonial Records Project microfilm,
Colonial Williamsburg. I am indebted to Professor J. D. Stewart for information about
Kneller and Jervas.

[3] Bridges's letter to Newman is quoted in Neale, "Charles Bridges," pp. 27–28. In his
account of the Bridges family, Thomas Wotton noted that Charles was twice-married.
The English Baronetage . . . , IV (London, 1741), pp. 188–190, cited in Neale, "Charles
Bridges," p. 7.

[4] Foote, "Charles Bridges," p. 10.

Bridges whom I take to be a very honest good man. He shall have all the encouragement I can give him."[5]

By December of that year Bridges had also met Colonel William Byrd II and had "drawn" his children "and several others in the neighbourhood," further eliciting from Byrd a letter of recommendation to former Lieutenant Governor Alexander Spotswood, who was then living in Spotsylvania County. In the same month Bridges acted as witness to the will of Sir John Randolph in Williamsburg. With such a splendid example of patronage from the governor and such a glittering array of contacts, it is difficult to see how the painter could have gone wrong.[6]

The warm reception accorded Bridges by these leaders of Virginia society betokens either an impressive reputation on his part or a strong desire on theirs to have their countenances immortalized and raise the tone of society by adopting a worthy painter. Byrd's letter to Spotswood tends to confirm the latter suppositions:

> The person who has the honour to wait upon you with this letter is a man of Good Family, but either by the frowns of Fortune or his own Mismanagement, is obliged to seek his Bread a little of the latest in a strange land. His name is Bridges, and his Profession is Painting and if you have any Employment for him in that way he will be proud of obeying your commands. He has drawn my children, and several others in the neighbourhood; and tho' he have not the Masterly Hand of a Lilly, or a Kneller, yet had he lived so long ago as when places were given to the most Deserving, he might have pretended to be the Sergeant-Painter of Virginia.[7]

If, however, the force of Byrd's sentiments arouses the suspicion that Bridges was especially welcome because Virginians had up to that

---

[5] James Blair to Bishop Gibson, July 7, 1735, Bishop of London Correspondence, Fulham Palace Papers, Lambeth Palace Library, copy, Virginia Colonial Records Project microfilm, Colonial Williamsburg.

[6] Foote, "Charles Bridges," p. 11.

[7] Ibid.

time existed in an artistic vacuum, the evidence strongly suggests that this was not so; indeed, an academic painter of a quality quite comparable to Bridges appears to have been active in the tidewater region in the 1720s.[8]

Whatever Bridges's artistic pretensions were, he wasted little time in exploring alternative ways of establishing himself in the New World, especially continuing the work of charity schools in which he was well versed. A few months after his arrival, Bridges was in correspondence with the Bishop of London, thanking him for his letter of recommendation and submitting a proposal for setting on foot "a Charity . . . for teaching these poor Ignorant Souls [Negroes] the principles and Duties of Christianity." Bridges obviously had a managerial turn of mind (he seems earlier to have written a paper entitled "Methods for Management of Free Schools"), for his letter to the Bishop suggested that the latter recommend the Negro school

---

8 "Isham Randolph" (Virginia Historical Society, Richmond) is dated 1724 on the back of the canvas; it has been considered an English portrait (National Gallery of Art, *The Eye of Thomas Jefferson* [Washington, D. C., 1976], pp. 5–6), an attribution that I question. A portrait of "William Randolph" was painted in 1729 at the age of 46, and was subsequently copied by Wollaston in 1755; the original has disappeared but the Wollaston copy is clearly marked on the back of the canvas, Virginia Historical Society. Even allowing for Wollaston's quite different style, the two portraits of "Isham" and "William Randolph" have strong similarities. Also during this period (1727), Robert "King" Carter "sat to the painter" at his house, Corotoman, Lancaster County, but, with egregious disregard for historians, omitted to say who the painter was. Robert "King" Carter Diary, 1722–1727, Alderman Library, University of Virginia, Charlottesville, microfilm, Colonial Williamsburg. It is not known which portrait this might be. "King" Carter had listed two other portraits of himself a year earlier when he drew up his will. Perhaps the likeliest candidate for the 1727 portrait is that reputed to be of "King" Carter at Sabine Hall; unfortunately, it is so heavily overpainted that it is impossible at present to determine its similarity in technique to the aforementioned portraits. The portrait reputed to be of "King" Carter at Shirley, which is discussed later in this work, does not resemble the two Randolph portraits at all. Perhaps the portrait of *John Bolling, Sr.* (College of William and Mary) also belongs to this group.

If the painter of these portraits was in the habit of dating them (at least two of them are), it is possible that he had also painted a portrait of John Custis in 1725 and so dated it. I have suggested later in this essay that the portrait of *John Custis IV* (Washington and Lee University) is a Bridges copy of an earlier portrait, which Bridges had dated—in highly unusual and distinctive fashion—on the front of the canvas to leave no doubt about its earlier origin.

According to his diary (August 31, 1727), "King" Carter had only two visitors to his

to the "great Merchants trading to Virginia" who might subscribe to it, then to Commissary Blair, who in turn would recommend it to the governor, which would ensure the success of the project.[9] The idea did not originate with Bridges, however, for the Bishop had in 1727 sent a pastoral letter "To the Masters and Mistresses of Families in the English Plantations abroad; Exhorting them to encourage and Promote the Instruction of their Negroes in the Christian Faith." Unfortunately, the proposals came to nothing. Exactly three years later Bridges wrote to Bishop Gibson from Hanover County:

household that he considered worthy of note the day he "sat to the painter." He had actually been urged to have his picture taken some days earlier by Colonel Page, his son-in-law, which might suggest that the two portraits mentioned in his will of 1726 showed him at different stages of life. His two visitors were "Mr. Jones" and Charles Stagg. The exact entry reads: "Mr. Jones came here last Night Stag came here abt 11 I sat to the Painter."

Charles Stagg had been a frequent visitor to Corotoman, in contact with Carter from at least 1722. He had been in the colony since 1715 when he and his wife were indentured to William Levingston, merchant and owner of a "peripatetic dancing school" in New Kent County. Stagg was listed as a "Dancing Master," and was such a talented individual that he was soon released from his indenture and entered into partnership with Levingston to operate a newly erected theater in Williamsburg, the first in the colonies. He also continued to run the dancing school. In fact, despite the ambitious nature of the theater's beginning—when Levingston had "at his own proper Cost and Charge sent to *England* for Actors and Musicians for the better Performance of the sd. Plays," and Governor Spotswood had inaugurated it—Stagg's dancing classes kept him from the desperate financial condition into which Levington quickly descended. Quotation in Hugh F. Rankin, *The Theater in Colonial America* (Chapel Hill, N. C., 1960), p. 12. "King" Carter frequently paid Stagg for his help with balls, "Assemblys," and plays, but never mentioned him again in context with portrait painting. Stagg died very shortly after Bridges's arrival in Williamsburg, having attained financial security and an established position. There is nothing in his inventory to suggest further that he might have painted portraits.

[9] Charles Bridges to Bishop Gibson, October 20, 1735, Fulham Palace Papers: "As your kind letter to your Comissary here on my behalf, procured me many favours from him for which I am principally obliged to your goodness, so it was with a peculiar pleasure I met with your pastoral letter to the Masters and owners of the Negroes here for promoting and Encouraging their Instruction in the Christian Faith. For having upon discourse with several of them found a good disposition to receive such Instruction it appears to me as great a Charity to set a proposal on foot for teaching these poor Ignorant Souls the principles and Duties of Christianity as it was formerly for setting up Charity Schools for the Children of the poor in London and several other parts. The beginning of which I was very well acquainted with. The Inclosed therefore is with due submission offer'd to your Consideration and being approved, It is hoped you will of your great goodness

The little Good I find I am Capable of doing without your particular Countenance in first Subscribing and Getting Subscriptions to that your Excellent design of Instructing the Negroes here according to the Method proposed. and pressing the Comissary to follow you and to Sollicit the Governor and his Interest I say all that can be done in this affair without your Charitable Efforts will to my great Concern I fear come to Nothing. The Comissary and I grow in years, And the World hangs heavy upon us. I am roused Sometimes and then call upon him. And then he is asleep perhaps and

recomend the design among the great Merchants trading to Virginia, some of which may very probably subscribe to it, and then to your Comissary here for him to introduce it to the Governor a person of an Excellent Spirit, who giving me great Countenance here and admitting me to his Conversation I have reason to believe will and Encourage this Charity, and when once it has beginning at Williamsburg, I doubt not of seeing the progress of it in other parts of this Country and Maryland especially where the Clergy are to be influenced by your Goodness to bestirr themselves heartily in this pious affair and as to my own part I shall be glad to do any thing that is in my power to further it, and wish now I had sought for a Character when I had the opportunity, that might more effectually have helped me to promote it. But since I have no other design in this but the good of human Nature I hope by the direction of so good a Guide as my Bishop, my labour will not be in vain."

Bridges's proposals accompanied his letter: "Whereas several Comendable Charity's have of late years been promoted in Great Brittain, particularly that of Instructing poor Children in the principles of Religion; which Succeeded so well that great Numbers of Schools have been Erected there for poor Boys and Girls, wherein many Thousands have been Educated to usefull and pious purposes, and out of which Some hundreds every year have been put to Service and apprenticeships, To the Children great Advantage both Temporal and Spiritual for the honour of the Christian Religion and the Satisfaction of the persons Concern'd in Contributing toward that Charitable design.

And whereas many poor Ignorant Souls among the Negroes in these parts of America do very much want and several of them desire to be Instructed in the principles and duties of a Christian life as well after as before they are Baptiz'd.

And the Rt. Revd. the Bishop of London having express'd his great Concern for these very people and their Children in his pastoral letter not long ago directed to the Masters and owners of Such Negroes; wherin he earnestly exhorts them to Encourage and promote the Instruction of them in the Christian [*illeg.*]

And Sunday being generally allow'd these poor Slaves as a day of Liberty to do many things for themselves and for spending that time for their own advantage.

It is therefore humbly proposed to the Honble. the Governor, the Revd. the Comissary and other Gentlemen and Inhabitants of Williamsburg that they wou'd please to Encourage the Instruction in this place by the following method.

1. By agreeing to have a Sermon every first Sunday and Catechizing every 2d Sunday afternoon in the month for carrying on the said Charitable Design.

answers nothing, and I am ready to Sleep too. Would to God your powerfull voice woud sound it in our ears to get up and be doing a little more Good. This Good work, while there is time and opportunity, which woud incite us to be thankfull to your Goodness for so great a blessing and especially to me.[10]

Bridges appears to have been putting a benign interpretation on the whole matter, for the lack of progress probably came at least as much from the "Masters' and Mistresses'" skepticism as it did from Blair's and his increasing age and lethargy. Blair had put his weight behind the Bishop's exhortations from the first, but the real threat of a slave rebellion in 1730—fueled by rumors that Spotswood was returning from England with orders from George II to free baptized slaves— crushed his hopes. Blair wrote the Bishop in 1731, "Not withstanding all the precaution we Ministers took to assure them that Baptism altered nothing as to their Servitude, or other temporal circumstances; yet they were willing to feed themselves with a secret fancy that it did, and that the King designed that all Christians should be made free." The Negroes "grew angry and saucy, and met in the

---

2. By Subscribing what every one pleases to contribute Quarterly toward the Charge of Such a Sermon and Catechizing.

3. By meeting every third Sunday or other day once a Month to Consult abt managing and promoting this good design and for keeping Accots. of the money received and applying it to the uses intended.

4. By using proper means and Argumts to Engage the Revd. Minister or Ministers Imploy'd on these Occasions to preach on Such Subjects and Catechize in Such a plain affecting way as may move their hearers to be Concern'd for the Instruction of these poor Souls and to have a Sincere love for the Christian Religion.

5. By Settling a Constant Master or Catechist if the Subscriptions arise and are Sufficient, whose whole business shall be to receive and Encourage all the Negroes and their Children that come of themselves or are sent by their owner, and then (in the School to be fixed) Instructing them familiarly in the Christian principles and inculcating them so frequently till they understand and incline to perform their duty both to God and Man.

6. By Obliging this Master or Catechist to be always upon the Spot at reasonable hours to attend those that come to be Instructed at the times they can be spared, and to make it his whole business to teach the Negroes and no other."

[10] Bridges to Bishop Gibson, October 19, 1738, Fulham Palace Papers.

night time in great numbers, and talked of rising; and in some places of choosing their leaders."[11] Gooch also corresponded with the Bishop about the "Insurrection": "What your Lordship observes is of some Masters very true, they use their Negroes no better than their Cattle. And I can see no help for it: tho' far the greater number, having kind Masters, live much better than our poor labouring Men in England."[12] It seems obvious that whatever the owners of slaves thought about their Christian duty, the realities of the slave economy dictated strict control rather than fostering notions in the slaves "that some time or other Christianity will help them to their freedom."[13]

Bridges's activities in Virginia can be traced only sketchily in the written records. In the winter of 1735–1736 he presumably journeyed from Westover to Germanna, Spotswood's residence. The following summer Bridges's daughter Mary died in Bruton parish on August 24. In December 1736, through the agency of Henry Hacker, Bridges rented Greenhill in Williamsburg from the estate of Richard King for a period of twelve months. On April 28, 1737, Bridges again witnessed the will of Sir John Randolph, this time as it was being probated. After the lease for Greenhill expired, Bridges moved to Hanover County, through which he may have traveled in the previous year, for he had an account with Thomas Partridge, a Hanover merchant. In February 1738 he advertised in William Parks's *Virginia Gazette*:

> Whereas one Box, mark'd C.B. about 4 Feet square, and 14 Inches deep; and one other Box, mark'd C.B. about 5 Feet long 1 Foot wide, and 1 Foot deep, were brought By Capt. Bolling from England, last Year, for the Subscriber, living in Hanover County, and cannot

---

[11] Blair to Bishop Gibson, May 14, 1731, Fulham Palace Papers. See also Neale, "Charles Bridges," p. 49.

[12] William Gooch to Bishop Gibson, May 28, 1731, Fulham Palace Papers; Neale, "Charles Bridges," p. 50.

[13] The quotation is from Blair to Bishop Gibson, June 28, 1729, Fulham Palace Papers; Neale, "Charles Bridges," p. 47.

be heard of by him: These are to request the Favour of the Person who has them in Possession, to give Notice to Him, or to the Printer hereof, where they are, and they shall be handsomely satisfy'd for their Trouble, by Charles Bridges.

As the boxes correspond in size to standard portraits of the period, one might surmise that the long box contained stretchers and rolled canvas, while the square one held frames and perhaps even some finished paintings, for several of the portraits attributed to Bridges, including those of members of the Bolling family, have identical carved and gilded frames of the period.[14]

From 1738 to 1740 Bridges's name appears several times in Hanover County records, mainly in accounts with merchants. During this time he also visited Belvoir, the house of William Fairfax in Prince William County, where he signed the guest book; Westover, in Charles City County, where he dined twice with William Byrd II, who referred to him as "old Bridges"; and Caroline County, for the courthouse of which he painted the royal arms, being paid "after the same rate [1,000 lbs. of tobacco] he hath been paid by other County Courts." He may also at this time have painted portraits of the Moore family in King William County. Bridges still had children living with him, for their names are mentioned in accounts for clothes in 1739 and 1740.[15]

From 1740 to 1743 Bridges's name appears with less frequency. He brought a case before the Charles City County court in 1741/2 and still had an account with Francis Jerdone, a merchant of Hanover County, in October 1743. If the portrait called *Mrs. Mann Page II and child* is indeed of that lady and was painted by Bridges, it indicates that Bridges was in the Williamsburg area in the winter of 1743–1744, for the Pages' first child was not born until April 1743, and the portrait does not show a child much under one year of age. It is

---

[14] Neale, "Charles Bridges," pp. 34–36; Foote, "Charles Bridges," pp. 12–13.
[15] Neale, "Charles Bridges," pp. 36–40; Foote, "Charles Bridges," pp. 13–14.

a remarkable coincidence that between May 1744 and May 1745 "1 large hair trunk with about 200 prints" and "1 paint box" were acquired by William Dering, who, it appears, established himself as Bridges's successor in the Williamsburg area in the matter of painting portraits. It may well be that Dering acquired these items from the departing painter.[16]

No later record of Bridges in Virginia is known. Exactly when he left the colony is unclear, but it is definite—as family tradition has it—that he returned to England to die. He was buried at Warkton, near Barton Seagrave, Northamptonshire, on December 18, 1747; his age was given as seventy-seven. The name "Charles Bridges" also appears in a notebook of George Vertue, the London engraver and antiquarian, in a mid-1746 context: "For Mr. Charles Bridges to Tho. Martin at Palgrave in Suffolk near Dis in Norfolk." Vertue's well-known connection with the arts and artists of the period makes it a reasonable guess that this was the same man.[17]

⚔

Bridges's career as an artist in England was unexceptional, to judge by the records he left. No signed or dated paintings survive; in fact, there is firm evidence for only one commission—that of the Reverend Thomas Baker, fellow of St. John's College, Cambridge, from 1680 until 1717, when he was ejected from his fellowship because he was a nonjuror.[18] A mezzotint of Baker by J. Simon (Fig. 1), published by Thomas Bakewell in Fleet Street, London, bears the unusual inscription "Cars. Bridges pinxit memoriter," which might be translated "Charles Bridges painted it from memory." The inscription

---

[16] Neale, "Charles Bridges," pp. 41–43. See also p. 101 of this study.

[17] Neale, "Charles Bridges," pp. 57–58; Foote, "Charles Bridges," pp. 14–15; Thorne, "Charles Bridges, Limner," p. 25.

[18] A nonjuror disclaimed allegiance to the Hanoverian succession. This was of particular concern after the Jacobite uprising of 1715.

FIGURE 1. *Rev. Thomas Baker*, engraved by John Simon after Charles Bridges.

12

further records the fact that Baker was a "Late Fellow" of St. John's College, thus dating the portrait after 1717.[19]

Five painted versions of the portrait of Baker exist which, because no Virginia portrait signed by Bridges was previously known, have been thoroughly discussed in the past. The Oxford version (Fig. 2) has generally been regarded as the original and would appear to be the one from which the mezzotint was made; indeed, the unusual inscription on the mezzotint was once associated with this version. In an eighteenth-century life of Baker, it was stated that the portrait "was purchased out of Lord Oxford's Collection by Dr. Rawlinson [1742] and placed in the Picture Gallery at Oxford [1745]. Charles Bridges pinxit memoriter."[20] However, the author of this biography, in his *Catalogue of the . . . pictures in the . . . Colleges . . . of Cambridge*, which he wrote six years after the biography, noted two portraits of Baker at St. John's, one "Thomas Baker, B.D." in the master's "Dressing Room," and the other "Mr. Thomas Baker, Oval, by Bridges" in the college hall. Of the three portraits of Baker now at St. John's, the one at present shown in the upper library corresponds best with the description of the latter (Fig. 3); the oval shape is clearly visible and has obviously been pieced out into a rectangle.[21]

---

19 The British Museum version of the mezzotint illustrated in Fig. 1 does not include the inscription, which is given in full in John Chaloner Smith, *British Mezzotinto Portraits*, III (London, 1880), p. 1068. See also n. 2.

20 Robert Masters, *Life of Thomas Baker* (Cambridge, 1784), quoted in R. Lane Poole, *Catalogue of Portraits in . . . Oxford*, I (Oxford, 1902), pp. 96–97.

21 J. W. Goodison, former deputy director of the Fitzwilliam Museum, Cambridge, also made this observation in his manuscript catalogue description of the portrait (courtesy of N. C. Buck, St. John's College Library). A small version also exists at the Society of Antiquaries, London, given in 1766 by a vice president, James West. It is smaller (20" x 18") than the others, which are the standard 30" x 25" size. G. Scharf, first secretary, and later director, National Portrait Gallery, London, described it as the original in his catalogue of the portraits at the Society of Antiquaries, 1865. If this is not complicated enough, George Vertue also "drew the picture of old Mr. Baker of St. John's" when he was in Cambridge in July 1729, accompanied by Lord Oxford, to whom Baker later bequeathed most of his manuscripts. Is it possible that Bridges based his painting, from which John Simon made the mezzotint, on the drawing by Vertue, which is now at the Lewis–Walpole Library, Farmington, Connecticut? See also Thorne, "Charles Bridges, Limner," p. 22, and Neale, "Charles Bridges," pp. 23–26.

FIGURE 2. *Rev. Thomas Baker*, attributed to Charles Bridges.

14

FIGURE 3. *Rev. Thomas Baker*, attributed to Charles Bridges.

Because of the questions concerning these portraits, they are not an ideal tool with which to tackle the complicated problem of the colonial portraits. Even if both the Bodleian and the St. John's portraits are by Bridges, they do not provide enough parallels with the portraits of Virginians here attributed to him to be vitally important to this study. After all, there may be as much as an eighteen-year interval between the portraits of Baker and the Virginia portraits, which could cause rather than dispel confusion. Of much greater concern to the present study is the material directly related to Bridges's portraits in Virginia that survives the difficult passage between the Scylla of hallowed (and frequently inaccurate) family tradition and the Charybdis of an often predetermined (and insufficient) scrutiny of the visual evidence.

Of central importance to the task of identifying Bridges's Virginia paintings is the portrait of *Mrs. Mann Page II and child* (Fig. 4). It was given to the College of William and Mary, together with the companion portrait of *Mann Page II*, by Dr. R. C. M. Page, the donor of an important group of Page family portraits in 1897. On the back of the replaced stretcher of this painting is the inscription "ALICE GRYMES/First wife of Mann Page II married 1743/*Chas. Bridges fecit*" (Fig. 5).[22] This important inscription, containing the only known "signature" of Bridges on a Virginia portrait, seems not to have been noticed before, or if it has, it has never been given its proper due.

For a number of reasons, the inscription, as it appears at present, probably dates from sometime in the last two decades of the nineteenth century. It was written with a brush in red wash on an unusual type of stretcher—incorporating two horizontal medial strips, with the resulting three spaces filled with solid wooden panels—that is

---

[22] Dr. R. Channing M. Page was accumulating this group of portraits from at least 1878, and published two editions of *Genealogy of the Page Family in Virginia . . .* (New York, 1883, 1893); the portraits of Mann Page II and of his wife and child are not mentioned in either.

FIGURE 20. "Mrs. Ludwell and children," by Charles Bridges.

FIGURE 28. "Girls of the Grymes family," by Charles Bridges.

FIGURE 4. *Mrs. Mann Page II and child*, by Charles Bridges. See color plate facing page xvi.

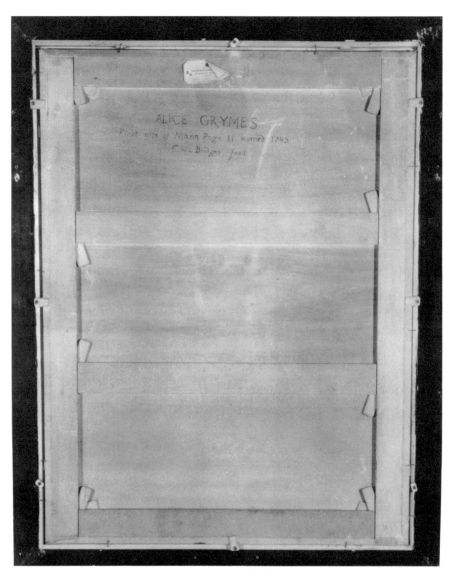

ALICE GRYMES
First wife of Mann Page II married 1743
Chas. Bridges fecit

FIGURE 5. Detail of reverse of Fig. 4.

common to a number of the portraits given to the college by Dr. Page. At least five of these stretchers carry the label of Beers Brothers, Broadway, New York, an artists' supply company active from about 1871. Three of the stretchers bear an inscription in a similar red wash, and in what is patently a late nineteenth-century calligraphy, that gives detailed information about the sitter and where, when, and from which Page family member Dr. Page purchased the picture. The three all include the words "Restored by Lauthier New York—1878"; two of them—"Jane Byrd Page" and "The Hon. John Page" —include the statement, in the same nineteenth-century writing, "Painted by Bridges about 1750." Only the inscription on the back of *Mrs. Mann Page II and child* has what is an obvious copy of an eighteenth-century signature that closely resembles Bridges's own (Fig. 6). It is unreasonable to think that such a signature was added for dubious commercial reasons; in the 1880s and 1890s Bridges was almost completely unknown outside of family tradition, and his signature certainly not available.[23]

Until such time as the relining canvas is removed and the back of the original canvas is revealed, one can only presume that the signature visible at present is an honest copy of the original signature by Bridges. Yet it must be conceded that the above argument, convincing or not, would seem perhaps too tenuous a thread of reasoning upon

[23] Mann Page II (1718–1778) and Alice Grymes (1724–1746) were actually married in December 1741, not 1743 as the inscription states; it was their first child who was born in 1743. This factual error is found in both editions of Dr. Page's genealogy; he may well have caused it to be put on the stretcher, because that part of the inscription does not seem to be in the eighteenth-century style, as the signature definitely is. Bridges's name does not appear in William Dunlap, *A History of the Rise and Progress of the Arts of Design in the United States* (New York, 1834), the basic and indispensable survey of early American painting; only in the edition revised by Frank W. Bayley and Charles E. Goodspeed (Boston, 1918) does an account of his career appear in the bibliography for the first time, and even then in little more than a token way, a characteristic of subsequent surveys. Even though Dunlap lived in Norfolk, Virginia, for three successive winters, 1819–1822, and visited plantations including Westover—by then, of course, emptied of its eighteenth-century contents—he did not note Bridges's work. Ibid., pp. 277–288. It would seem that Bridges's fame, such as it was, had by then evaporated.

SIGNATURES OF CHARLES BRIDGES

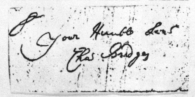

BEFORE 1730: Charles Bridges to Richard Roach, no date,
Rawlinson Papers, D. 832, f. 45, Department
of Western Manuscripts, Bodleian Library,
Oxford, England.

1735: Charles Bridges to Bishop Gibson, Williamsburg,
October 20, 1735, Bishop of London Correspondence -
Fulham Palace Papers, 15, f. 40.

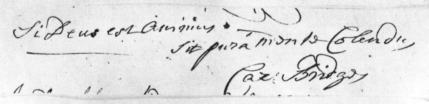

BETWEEN 1737 AND 1739: "Belvoir House Guest Book," Virginia
Historical Society, Richmond, Virginia. Foote, "Charles
Bridges," Virginia Magazine of History and Biography,
LX (1952), 13.

1738: Charles Bridges to Bishop Gibson, Hanover, October 19,
1738, Bishop of London Correspondence - Fulham Palace
Papers, 15, f. 47.

FIGURE 6. Signatures of Charles Bridges, ca. 1725–1739.

which to place the burden of proof for attributing a significant group of portraits, were it not for the fact that the portrait of *Mrs. Mann Page II and child*, and the companion portrait of *Mann Page II* (Fig. 11), which is a powerful and memorable picture, bear a striking resemblance in appearance and technique to two portraits of children of the Byrd family that Thomas Thorne has previously assigned to Bridges.[24] A certain similarity (to judge from photographs) between the head of Mrs. Page and that of the Reverend Baker (Fig. 3) can also be noted.

Bridges had "drawn" the children of William Byrd II, as the latter wrote Spotswood in December 1735, although it is impossible to know which of his six children Byrd meant—Evelyn (b. 1707), Wilhemina (b. 1715), Anne (b. 1725), Maria (b. 1727), William III (b. 1728), and Jane (b. 1729). By his use of the word "children," Byrd may have intended to exclude his two daughters by his first wife, both of whom were of marriageable age. Portraits of four of the children, not including Wilhemina and Jane, were at Westover in 1838.[25] While portraits popularly believed to be of each of the children now exist, Thorne narrowed down the Bridges attribution initially to two—"Anne Byrd" (Fig. 7), and "William Byrd III" (Fig. 9).

Anne Byrd was ten years old in 1735; the portrait illustrated here might be thought to show a younger child. This portrait hung at Brandon until it was acquired by Colonial Williamsburg. In a list of portraits at Upper Brandon and Lower Brandon compiled about 1870, three portraits of children of William Byrd II were specified, one being Anne—"Mrs. Nancy Carter of Cleves, when a child, sister

---

24 Thorne, "Charles Bridges, Limner," pp. 29–31.

25 Evelyn, Maria, Anne, and two of William Byrd III. The will of Mary Willing Byrd, widow of William Byrd III, was drawn up in 1813 and proved in the Charles City County court on April 20, 1814. "The Will of Mrs. Mary Willing Byrd, of Westover, 1813, with a List of the Westover Portraits," *Virginia Magazine of History and Biography*, VI (April 1899), pp. 346–358. The will provides detailed information about the paintings and furnishings then at Westover.

FIGURE 7. "Anne Byrd," by Charles Bridges.

FIGURE 8. Detail of Fig. 7.

to the last Col. Byrd."[26] The portraits had presumably come to Brandon through the marriage of William Byrd III's daughter, Evelyn Taylor Byrd, to Benjamin Harrison of Brandon, although in 1813 the two girls' portraits, then described by their married names, as "Aunt Carter" and "Aunt Maria Carter," had been bequeathed to Evelyn's brother, William Powell Byrd.[27]

The portrait known as "William Byrd III," who would have been seven years old in 1735, has an equally confusing provenance. Since at least the third quarter of the nineteenth century, it hung at Whitehall, Gloucester County, the home of Richard Corbin Byrd, direct grandson of William Powell Byrd. However, of the two portraits of William Byrd III mentioned in 1813, one was bequeathed to Maria Horsemanden Byrd, and the other "at full length" to Richard Willing Byrd, sister and brother of William Powell Byrd.[28] Despite the unclear provenance, however, it is certain that portraits of the chil-

---

[26] W. S. Morton, "The Portraits at Lower Brandon, and Upper Brandon, Virginia," *William and Mary Quarterly*, 2nd Ser., X (October 1930), pp. 338–340. Also at Brandon about 1870 was "Mrs. Molly Carter [Maria Byrd Carter, second wife of Landon Carter of Sabine Hall] sister to the last Colonel Byrd ¾." See p. 114. This list also includes "Miss Evelyn Byrd, Daughter of the 2d Col. Byrd, very handsome, hair plain, rose on her left side, ringlets flowing on her shoulders—died unmarried." Mary Willing Byrd had left to her daughter, Evelyn Taylor Byrd Harrison, "the portrait of her aunt Evelyn." The portrait owned by Colonial Williamsburg (1941-76) appears on the wall of the drawing room at Lower Brandon in Thomas Allen Glenn, *Some Colonial Mansions and Those Who Lived in Them*, I (Philadelphia, 1899), p. 417. It was inherited by Mrs. Stephen Decatur Mayo, the former Isabelle Ritchie Harrison, before its acquisition by Colonial Williamsburg. Mrs. Mary R. M. Goodwin has been of inestimable help in unraveling these mysteries.

[27] Although the disposition of the portraits according to Mary Willing Byrd's will was quite clear, at least eleven other portraits that were at Brandon about 1870 correspond exactly to those bequeathed to her sons, Charles, Richard, and William. Mary Willing Byrd might have foreseen some such transferal: "It is my will and desire, that if my said son [Charles Willing Byrd] shall find it inconvenient to carry these portraits to his house, that they shall be equally divided between his two brothers, Richard and William Byrd."

[28] Maria married John Page of Pagebrook in Frederick (now Clarke) County. The pictures she inherited were described as "the portrait of her honored father and one of myself [Mary Willing Byrd]," which suggests a pair of portraits of a period later than the one during which Bridges was active.

dren of William Byrd II have remained in the possession of various descendants until recent times. From the point of view of the history of ownership and the coincidence of the children's ages, the portraits of "Anne Byrd" and "William Byrd III" could well be the ones that Bridges had "drawn."

A visual comparison of the two child portraits with that of *Mrs. Mann Page II and child* (Fig. 4), reveals many similarities, taking into account the condition of the former—"Anne Byrd" has been somewhat overcleaned and gives the impression of having been flattened and smoothed, while "William Byrd III" has been grievously damaged and the central figure completely overpainted by an amateur using white-lead paint.[29] The two Byrd children were definitely painted by the same artist, in my opinion, and show obvious correspondences in the pose, in the handling of the drapery and the form of it as it flows from the child's left shoulder over the right thigh to fall on the ground, and in the awkward stance. Details of the background of the boy's portrait that have not been repainted (the upper left) are identical to details of the background in the companion portrait.

The head of Mrs. Page's child and that of "Anne Byrd" are exceptionally close in handling and character, given the latter's somewhat overcleaned condition.[30] The same shaping, shading, and highlighting of the mouth, nose, and eyes are evident, as are the same wispy hair and slight tilt to the head, and the same wooden hand and stance. A comparison of the red drapery of the Page child and the well-preserved blue drapery in the lower left corner of the portrait of "William Byrd III" (Fig. 10) reveals mannerisms consistent to one

---

[29] Thorne, "Charles Bridges, Limner," pp. 28–31. According to an inscription on the back of the (replaced) stretcher of "Anne Byrd," the portrait was "Restored May 1852." A stencil on the reverse of the relining canvas read as follows: "Waterproof lining and restoring by C. Volkman/So. Frederick St. No. 14 Baltimore." When the picture was restored in 1958, the reverse of this lining fabric was found to have been coated with a metal leaf and some areas of the figure had been repainted.

[30] Noted and described by Thorne in "Charles Bridges, Limner."

FIGURE 9. "William Byrd III," attributed to Charles Bridges.

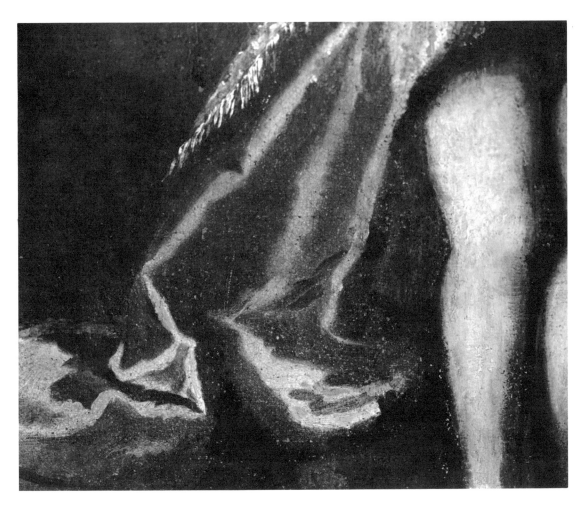

FIGURE 10. Detail of Fig. 9.

artist.[31] This drapery is highly indicative of Bridges's brushwork.

Mrs. Mann Page II and her husband (Fig. 11) are powerfully realized. As the portrayal of a physical presence, the picture of the man is more convincing, for the parts are better proportioned and coordinated; Mrs. Page's arms, waist, and knees seem to lack proper connection with the rest of her body. The satin of her dress demands bolder and more brilliant highlights than the velvet of his coat, but both give Bridges the opportunity for some bravura brushwork, especially in the area closest to the light source and the viewer. It is the heads, however, that rivet our attention (Figs. 12 and 13) with an uncompromising and, perhaps, even surly gaze. Although the eyes are not completely successfully aligned on the proper planes and levels, the parts of the faces are firmly modeled with precise brushwork, creating a characterization in each portrait that is convincing and memorable.

Colonial artists' dependence on late seventeenth- and early eighteenth-century English mezzotints, which provided novel and socially desirable poses, accessories, and backgrounds, has long been known. Indeed, the portrait of *Mrs. Mann Page II and child* was illustrated in the first complete study of this topic.[32] It is possible that the portraits of "Anne Byrd" and "William Byrd III" were based on a mezzotint such as Henri Gascars's *Charles Duke of Richmond and Lennox*, which shows a young aristocrat in antique garb accompanied by his black servant. Even more likely as a design source is the mezzotint of the *Hon. William Cecil* by John Smith after William Wissing (Fig. 14), which appears to have been one of a series of prints that were copied literally by a naive artist making portraits of the Jaquelin and Brodnax families of Jamestown probably in the

---

[31] Thorne gives a good illustration of the head of the black boy in the background of the portrait of "William Byrd III"; it has suffered some loss but has not been overpainted. Ibid. The handling of it, in my opinion, is quite consistent with other children's heads here ascribed to Bridges.

[32] Waldron Phoenix Belknap, Jr., *American Colonial Painting: Materials for a History* (Cambridge, Mass., 1959), p. 310, pl. 38.

1720s.[33] While such a fashion would have been a generation old in England in 1735 (and rather frayed at the edges), it probably appealed to William Byrd II as having been in style during his sojourn there. Because it lacks the mannered decorative devices of the mezzotints, but rather is presented in a natural and straightforward way, the portrait of *Mann Page II* is the most immediate and forceful of the group.[34]

Upon his arrival in Virginia, Bridges had received assurances of support and encouragement from the two most influential men in the colony, William Gooch and James Blair. Indeed, Gooch had specifically promised to commission a portrait of himself; if such a portrait was completed, it has since disappeared. Two portraits thought to be of James Blair have survived, the larger one being owned by the College of William and Mary presumably since Blair's death in 1743. Although the portraits were described as "Rev. John Blair" in the mid-nineteenth century (and the smaller one elsewhere called "Hugh Blair"),[35] the iconography of the larger portrait (Fig.

---

[33] Edward Jaquelin, Jr. (Mary Black, "The Case Reviewed," *Arts in Virginia*, X [fall 1969], Fig. 5) is a direct use of the Smith/Wissing composition, as "Rebeckah Brodnax" (ibid., Fig. 7) is of Smith's mezzotint of John Medina's *Ann Roydhouse* (Belknap, *American Colonial Painting*, Fig. 41). Other correspondences were noted in Mary Black, "The Case of the Red and Green Birds," *Arts in Virginia*, III (winter 1963), pp. 3–9. The mezzotint after Gascars is reproduced in Smith, *British Mezzotinto Portraits*, III, p. 527.

If, however, the Jaquelin–Brodnax–Ambler group does not belong to the 1720s—and there is scant evidence to prove that it does—perhaps we might consider it in relation to Peter Wagener, resident in Virginia 1705–1707, who was described by no less than Governor Gooch, in a letter to the Bishop of London: "I am persuaded your Lordship will be surprised when I declare upon the Testimony of Gentlemen, who have equally at heart the Interest of Religion, that the Person I am speaking of, is much better remembered here as a bad Painter, than as a Divine." May 21, 1739, Fulham Palace Papers. See also n. 50.

[34] Virgil Barker, *American Painting: History and Interpretation* (New York, 1950), pp. 102–106, chose *Mann Page II* as the sole illustration in his discussion of Bridges—not that he gave any evidence to prove that the portrait was by him.

[35] The mention of two portraits of "John Blair" comes from the faculty minutes of November 22, 1859, describing the Wren Building at the College of William and Mary as it was before the fire of that year. E. G. Swem, "Some Notes on the Four Forms of the Oldest Building of William and Mary College," *William and Mary Quarterly*, 2nd

FIGURE 11. *Mann Page II*, by Charles Bridges. For color plate, see frontispiece.

FIGURE 12. Detail of Fig. 11.

FIGURE 13. Detail of Fig. 4.

FIGURE 14. *Hon. William Cecil*, by John Smith after William Wissing.

FIGURE 15. *James Blair*, by Charles Bridges.

34

15) leaves no doubt that it represents the commissary to the Bishop of London in the colony of Virginia and president of the College of William and Mary, James Blair. Unfortunately, it has been badly abraded, particularly in the area of the face and figure. Despite the damage, however, there are enough similarities of handling between it and the portrait of Mann Page II—especially in the structure of the head and hands—as well as enough documented connections between Bridges and Blair, to make the attribution to Bridges a persuasive one.

With its extended imagery, this portrait is Bridges's most ambitious work—at the commissary's insistence almost certainly, for he was not a modest man. Bridges followed a well-established compositional formula to portray this powerful ecclesiastic, namely, a three-quarter length seated figure, a Bible near him on a table, and a view of the principal seat of his power (normally, of course, a cathedral) through a window to his right.[36] Blair, who was about eighty years old at the time he met Bridges, is shown full-face, his arm resting on a table upon which is a Bible, in Greek, open to the Sermon on the Mount from the Gospel according to St. Matthew. Blair's own collection of sermons, a five-volume exegesis entitled *Our Saviour's Divine Sermon on the Mount*, had been published in London in 1722 under the sponsorship of the Society for Promoting Christian Knowledge, for which Bridges had been an agent several years earlier.[37]

Through the window behind Blair is seen one of the earliest views of the College of William and Mary as it was rebuilt after the disastrous fire of 1705. In the foreground, in front of the college, a

---

Ser., VIII (October 1928), p. 282. The smaller portrait mentioned in the faculty minutes may well be the one thought to have been painted by Hargreaves in London in 1705 (Parke Rouse, Jr., *James Blair of Virginia* [Chapel Hill, N. C., 1971], frontispiece), and not the one illustrated here (Fig. 15), which also appears in *A Memoir of a Portion of the Bolling Family in England and Virginia* (Richmond, Va., 1868), pp. 34–35, for which reference I am grateful to Parke Rouse, Jr. Hugh Blair was born in 1718, which would make him rather younger than the man in Fig. 16.

[36] See, for example, Selby Whittingham, "Some Portraits of Bishop Burnett around 1690," *Burlington Magazine*, CXVIII (September 1976), pp. 649–650.

[37] Rouse, *James Blair*, pp. 232–240.

phoenix rises from the ashes, an allusion not simply to the physical rebuilding of the college, 1709–1716, but also to the dramatic revitalization of the institution that had come about through Blair's leadership. In 1726 Blair had finally succeeded in procuring a substantial revenue for the college in the form of a liquor tax, which provided him with the means to recruit an experienced faculty from British universities, most of whom were in Williamsburg by 1729. In that year, furthermore, the college passed from ownership by the charter trustees to ownership by the president and masters. Blair's achievement actually constituted a rebirth for the college, and, characteristically, he saw to it that the painter did not overlook the matter.[38]

The angle from which the college is seen through the open window (from the southeast) means that Blair must have been sitting, not in the recently completed President's House, as long tradition has it, but in the Brafferton, the Indian school. Obviously, this distinction is important. The Brafferton was an exceptional example of the charity school movement in the colonies, a result of the piety and charity of the great scientist, Robert Boyle. In his will of 1691, Boyle had directed funds "towards the propagating the Christian religion among infidels." From land acquired by his executors in Yorkshire— the manor of Brafferton—revenues were assigned, in large part, "for the advancement of the christian religion in Virginia." Blair may well have influenced the decision of the executors, one of whom was the Bishop of London, that the College of William and Mary administer these funds; with them "a good house and Apartments" for the "Educacon . . . of Indian Children" was constructed at the college in 1723. Bridges's own commitment to the charity schools in England, together with his and Blair's professed ambition to found another charity school in Virginia, this one for Negro children, would seem to have made the choice of the Brafferton—an exemplar for all

---

[38] Ibid., pp. 207–218.

in Virginia to behold—as the setting for Blair in his portrait a foregone conclusion.[39]

What at first sight, therefore, seems an unassuming portrait (and, because of its condition, it must be confessed, a somewhat unprepossessing one) is found to contain, to an unusual degree, a series of allusions emanating from the theme of Christian charity, embracing concepts of Christian education and leadership, and culminating in the meeting of sitter and artist on the common ground of their deeply humanitarian instincts. Although the visual devices that the painter used are disarmingly simple, the layers of reference are, for early colonial portraiture, quite complex. From the most sublime statement of Christian charity, Blair's lengthy commentary on which was sponsored by the charitable and religious organization that Bridges had been deeply involved with, through the manifold aspects of charity on an intellectual plane to children of the underprivileged, in which both men had been influential, the allusions spread to concepts of intellectual and social service on the highest levels, in which the sitter had distinguished himself and to which the artist was by nature attuned.

The smaller portrait that has in recent times been called "James Blair" (Fig. 16) is in much better condition, although still somewhat abraded in the face. A fresh and stimulating picture in spite of its yellowed varnish, it gives us an excellent idea of how Bridges's capabilities must have appeared and appealed to Virginians. It also provides a firm visual link between the large portrait of James Blair and that of Mann Page II, for when the three pictures are viewed together there is little doubt that they are the work of one painter. However, it is difficult to see how the smaller portrait can represent James Blair. With his slender oblong face (Fig. 17), in contrast to the puffy rounded features of the large portrait, the sitter is patently a different and younger individual despite the many similarities of handling in

---

[39] Marcus Whiffen, *The Public Buildings of Williamsburg* (Williamsburg, Va., 1958), pp. 106–112, quotations on pp. 106 and 107.

FIGURE 16. "John Blair," by Charles Bridges.

FIGURE 17. Detail of Fig. 16.

the nose, mouth, and structure of the eyes. Although, as already noted, the sitter was at one time identified as "Hugh Blair," it is suggested that he could be James's nephew John, in whose family, according to tradition, the portrait descended. As deputy auditor general of the colony and a member of the House of Burgesses, John Blair was prominent enough to have his portrait painted, and was about forty-eight years old at the time Bridges arrived in Williamsburg, quite consistent with the vigor we see portrayed.[40]

Since Alexander Spotswood had had Bridges recommended to him by no less a personage than William Byrd II, and since the former governor of the colony was not insensitive to pictures (and not beyond a little vanity, either), it is reasonable to presume that a portrait was commissioned.[41] Two similar portraits long said to be of Spotswood were owned by various members of the family for generations. One was given to the Commonwealth of Virginia in 1874, and the

---

[40] Illustrated in Rouse, *James Blair*, who notes that, according to tradition, the portrait was owned by Elizabeth Blair. John Blair had a half-sister, Elizabeth.

[41] In Spotswood's inventory of 1742, for example, appears "One Scripture peice of painting, the History of the Woman taken in adultery." "Inventory of the effects belonging to the estate of the late Gen. Spotswood," January 26, 1741/2, Orange County Records, Will Book No. 1, 1735-1743, p. 181, Virginia State Library, Richmond, copy, Colonial Williamsburg. At £36, it was valued higher even than the slaves and the horses, which is most extraordinary. No other mention of paintings is made in his inventory, but neither, for example, is his plate listed, described in his will as "two Cabinets of plate, weighing One thousand and Eighty nine ounces and four penny weight of silver." Ibid., p. 135.

Spotswood is the last prominent colonial personage discussed here who is known, through the documents, to have had a connection with Bridges, with the exception of Sir John Randolph. As one of the foremost men of his time in colonial society, Sir John was probably seen by Bridges, upon his arrival in Virginia, as an attractive possibility for a commission. Although no portrait has survived, a present descendant of the Randolph family owns daguerreotypes (silver-types?) said to have been made of miniature copies of portraits of Sir John and Lady Randolph. Despite the various copying processes involved, the lady in particular bears a very strong resemblance to other female portraits here attributed to Bridges, especially *Mrs. Mann Page II*, "Mrs. Lee," and "Mrs. Ludwell." The daguerreotypes were taken by James E. McClees of Philadelphia, active from 1843 to 1887, who is reputed to have been the first to use the photographic process in that city. Family tradition further holds that full-sized portraits did exist, but were destroyed in a fire at Hickory Hill, Hanover County, in 1875.

other was acquired by Colonial Williamsburg in 1940.[42] The latter (Fig. 18) descended in the possession of the Moore family of Chelsea, King William County, into which Spotswood's oldest daughter, Anna Catherina, had married (the same line of descent of five other portraits here attributed to Bridges). It, too, has suffered badly, the abrasion of the face resembling that of *James Blair*, while large areas of the costume—the richest of any of Bridges's male sitters—have been repainted. This damage has caused the kind of anatomical difficulties that Bridges sometimes experienced, already noted in the portrait of *Mrs. Mann Page II*, to become more prominent. In my opinion, the portrait of Spotswood owned by the Commonwealth of Virginia is not by Bridges. It might have been painted at any time up to one hundred years after the version discussed above, and even appears to show some of the damage which that version has sustained.

To portray the forceful military and administrative leader, Bridges chose a setting that was almost as visually ambitious as the one he had provided Blair, although some of the allusions are still hidden from us. Spotswood is seen standing before a fortified castle with a military encampment in the background. He had made his reputation as an officer with the Duke of Marlborough's army in the Low Countries, and was wounded at Blenheim, so it may well be that most important battle he wished to see represented in his portrait. He holds a scroll, now so badly damaged that it is blank; the later copy, however, shows an architectural plan in his hand. If this was Bridges's original intent, it would certainly be in character, for Spotswood had an absorbing interest in the creation or completion of appropriate architectural monuments in the New World, such as finishing the Capitol and Governor's Palace and rebuilding the college in Williamsburg; proposing the construction of a hospital and dock at Old Point Comfort; and building an ironworks at Germanna.

---

42 Foote, "Charles Bridges," pp. 30–31, attributed both portraits to Bridges. The example owned by the Commonwealth of Virginia hangs in the governor's mansion at Richmond.

FIGURE 18. *Alexander Spotswood*, by Charles Bridges.

The portraits already discussed thus form the basic group on which any further examination of paintings attributed to Bridges must depend, tying together as they do all the known (and reliable) documentary and traditional references to the painter and his patrons. Although the earliest portraits discussed date from the period 1735–1736 and the signed one to the end of Bridges's stay in the colonies, there is no discernible development in the painter's style, no evidence of progressive "Americanness." Considering his advanced age, we might presume that his style was set when he arrived and, consequently, susceptible mainly to decay.

As the one female portrait examined thus far is the only one signed and the number of portraits of men is exceeded by those of women and/or children, I will discuss this larger group first. Bearing a striking physical resemblance to *Mrs. Mann Page II* are portraits of "Hannah Ludwell Lee" (Fig. 19) and "Mrs. Ludwell and children" (Fig. 20), both in good condition and still owned by descendants of these families.[43] The smaller one shows a treatment of the drapery on shoulder and bust virtually identical to that of Mrs. Page. Compositionally, "Mrs. Ludwell" is closely allied to Mrs. Page, her left knee being foreshortened, however, to make way for the standing child. One notes the same stylized poses of the children and the same flaccid hands. "Mrs. Ludwell's" portrait has a more engaging color scheme, the white of the younger child's dress corresponding to the white of the mother's shift, both strongly contrasted to the rich blue of her gown and the primary red of the curtain to her right. The younger child has red, white, and blue flowers in her hair, while the older one's dress introduces a strong element of green, accentuated by the leaves and the peach. It is interesting to note a distinct blue penti-

---

[43] Hannah Ludwell was born in 1701, the daughter of Philip Ludwell of Greenspring, and married Thomas Lee of Stratford in Westmoreland County (see also n. 59). "Mrs. Ludwell and children" has traditionally been thought to be Frances Grymes Ludwell, wife of Philip Ludwell III of Greenspring, born 1717, married 1737, whose three daughters were born in 1737, 1740, and 1751. Foote, "Charles Bridges," pp. 38–39.

FIGURE 19. "Hannah Ludwell Lee," by Charles Bridges.

FIGURE 20. "Mrs. Ludwell and children," by Charles Bridges. See color plate facing page 16.

FIGURE 21. Detail of Fig. 20.

mento around the neckline of "Mrs. Lee's" dress, as if the blue robe were tied inside the silvery white dress.

One of Bridges's most charming pictures, a "Girl of the Ludwell family" (Fig. 22), accompanies the portrait of "Mrs. Ludwell and children." Evincing a strong family likeness to the older child in the large portrait, the young girl is fashionably attired in a rich blue dress with deeply scalloped bodice and red gown, and holds a basket of flowers containing a peony, a white rose and rosebud, and a blue morning glory (Fig. 24). She also has flowers in her hair—a pink rose, a blue iris(?), and white shadbush flowers. In this well-preserved portrait the bloom of young girlhood, the freshness of spring flowers, and the richness of sophisticated dress all harmonize, producing a delightful effect.

It should be noted, in view of Bridges's advertisement in 1738 for lost boxes, which probably contained frame moldings, that the frames of "Mrs. Lee" and the accompanying male portrait (Fig. 54), as well as the Bolling family group (Figs. 36, 38, and 59), are identical to those of "John Blair' and *Alexander Spotswood*, while the frames of the Ludwell portraits are more elaborate and identical to those of two double portraits of the Grymes children (Figs. 28 and 32).

One of the few Kit-Kat sized portraits attributed to Bridges is said to be "Mrs. William Randolph III," the wife of the man who built Wilton (Fig. 25).[44] She is shown in a typical Lely pose, wearing a pink dress with a blue robe and coral sleeve buttons, her elbow resting on a book on a table or ledge. The portrait has been damaged and is much in need of cleaning. The artistic likeness continues through smaller portraits of "Martha Page" (Fig. 26) and "Elizabeth Bolling Gay" (Fig. 27), the former having suffered badly at the hands

---

[44] Anne Harrison, daughter of Benjamin Harrison IV and Anne Carter, who married William Randolph III, was born ca. 1724, and by the time of Bridges's departure from Virginia would have been only 20 years old—much younger, it seems, than the woman seen here. Mrs. William (Elizabeth Beverley) Randolph II had died in 1723 at the age of 32. This is one of an important group of Randolph family portraits acquired by the Virginia Historical Society that now hangs at Wilton in Richmond.

FIGURE 22. "Girl of the Ludwell family," by Charles Bridges. See color plate facing page 1.

FIGURE 23. Detail of Fig. 22.

FIGURE 24. Detail of Fig. 22.

FIGURE 25. "Mrs. William Randolph III," by Charles Bridges.

FIGURE 26. "Martha Page," by Charles Bridges.

FIGURE 27. "Elizabeth Bolling Gay," by Charles Bridges.

of a "restorer" (an old photograph in the files of Colonial Williamsburg shows a much livelier and better preserved countenance), while the latter is one of an important group of portraits of the Bolling family to which reference will be made later.[45] Although the present whereabouts of the latter portrait is unknown, and it has not been examined, the attribution to Bridges on the basis of the photograph is made with some degree of certainty.

Bridges responded instinctively to children, if his portraits of the Byrd and Ludwell children are any indication. Indeed, the three double portraits of children that follow support this contention—for his child portraits alone Bridges should be regarded as one of the more endearing practitioners of the art of portraiture in the American colonies. Each of these double portraits is the conventional three-quarter (50 inches by 40 inches) size, but horizontal rather than vertical. The "Girls of the Grymes family" (Fig. 28) show obvious family and artistic kinship with the Ludwell children, and, again, utilize a Lely or Gascars compositional device. Once more the colors are intense and primary, although the dress of the younger child is pink and reminiscent of that of "Mrs. Randolph." Even the flowers in the basket are identical to those the Ludwell girl holds, while the landscape background resembles that in the Ludwell family group one suspects (if it could be seen clearly in the latter through the overlay of dirt). The "Boys of the Grymes family" (Fig. 32) could not but be from the same family! As with the girls, the artist has placed the older child, dressed in blue, on the left as the dominant point of

---

[45] "Martha Page" and the accompanying "Alice Page" (Fig. 55) were given to Colonial Williamsburg by Miss Mildred Nelson Page of Charlottesville in 1942. They were left to Miss Page by Dr. R. Channing M. Page of New York City (see p. 16 and n. 22), who had acquired them from the family of Thomas Jefferson Page of Shelly, Gloucester County, at some time after his gift of the group of Page family portraits to the College of William and Mary. Dr. Page believed Martha and Alice (b. 1693 and 1695) to be daughters of Matthew and Mary Mann Page; however, it appears that only one child, Mann, survived infancy. "Elizabeth Bolling Gay" was at one time recorded to be in the possession of Mrs. Robert Malcolm Littlejohn of New York City, who gave many of the Bolling family portraits to the College of William and Mary.

FIGURE 28. "Girls of the Grymes family," by Charles Bridges. See color plate facing page 17.

FIGURE 29. Detail of Fig. 28.

FIGURE 30. Detail of Fig. 28.

FIGURE 31. Detail of Fig. 28.

FIGURE 32. "Boys of the Grymes family," by Charles Bridges.

FIGURE 33. Detail of Fig. 32.

FIGURE 34. Detail of Fig. 32.

the composition, but it is the younger child who holds our attention with a riveting gaze. Comparison should also be made with the child in the portrait of *Mrs. Mann Page II* (Fig. 4), not only in the features but also in the broad, schematic quality of the rendition of the garment, not dissimilar to that of the older girl.[46]

"Two children of the Moore family" (Fig. 35) are somewhat older and are portrayed with a seriousness of mien that places them between the Grymes children and the portraits of adults. Actually, their physical features link them to portraits of adults still to be discussed rather than to the Grymes, Ludwell, and Byrd children. It is the only portrait in which Bridges endows his subjects with any sense of physical movement—it is as if the courtly young gentleman in his brilliant red suit, replete with his first sword, wig, and hat, were leading a fair companion through the estate to which he would one day fall heir. The richness of their station in life is conveyed by their adornments and the bold areas of primary colors.[47]

Among the portraits of men so far discussed, that of *Mann Page II* (Fig. 11) is in the best condition, with "John Blair" (Fig. 16) also providing a reliable basis for comparison. It is in relation to these that the unusually attractive portrait of *John Bolling, Jr.* (Fig. 36) can be attributed to Bridges; comparison with the older Grymes girl and boy (Figs. 28 and 32) must also be made. Because of its superior con-

---

[46] The four Grymes children have always been believed by the family to be children of John Grymes (1691–1748) and Lucy Ludwell Grymes (1698–1748) of Brandon in Middlesex County. There has been some confusion, however, about precisely which of their ten children are portrayed here—Hannah (b. 1717, married Dr. Henry Potter); John (1718–1740); Lucy (b. 1720, married Carter Burwell 1737); Philip (1721–1762); Charles (1723–1727); Alice (1724–1746); Benjamin (1725–1776); Sarah (1729–1731); Charles (1730–1732); and Ludwell (1733–1795). Alice, the youngest of the girls to survive infancy, became Mrs. Mann Page II and was painted by Bridges in her maturity. The boys could be Benjamin and Ludwell to judge by the ages of those in the portrait (courtesy of John M. Jennings).

[47] Tradition has it that they are Lucy and Bernard Moore, both born about 1720, children of Augustine (ca. 1685–1743) and Elizabeth Todd Seaton, who married ca. 1714. Bernard married Anna Catherina Spotswood sometime between 1740 and 1742, while Lucy married Speaker John Robinson about 1740.

FIGURE 35. "Two children of the Moore family," by Charles Bridges.

FIGURE 36. *John Bolling, Jr.*, by Charles Bridges. See color plate facing page 80.

FIGURE 37. Detail of Fig. 36.

dition, it is one of the most pleasing of the male portraits in its color harmonies of vivid blue coat, white shirt and wig, and pink complexion, as well as one of the most convincing in its sense of physical presence.

Bridges saw these Virginia gentry as serious and restrained, sober in their choice of fine materials for clothes, with only occasional touches of adornment, solid in their presence and uncompromising in their gaze. Characteristically, he gave them high, strong foreheads, made oval by the (often misaligned) wig set back, and accentuated by a bold highlight on the right side. The nose is generally long or heavy, the eyes imperfectly aligned, and the lips strongly shaped.

The female portrait accompanying that of *John Bolling, Jr.*, said to be his wife, *Elizabeth Blair Bolling* (Fig. 38), is abraded and flatter; while simply dressed, almost to the point of plainness, the lady still radiates a freshness and charm. Bridges had come into contact with the Bolling family not only through the sea captain who brought over his boxes—probably of artists' supplies—but also presumably through this lady, who was the niece of James Blair.[48]

From the portrait of *John Bolling, Jr.*, it is a very short step to that of *John Custis IV* (Fig. 40), whose surpassing interest in matters horticultural is indicated by the book in his left hand, lettered on the front edge "Of The Tulip," and by the large cut tulip lying nearby.[49] However striking the physical similarities are, the relationship is complicated by the inscription on the upper left front of the latter, "AETAT 48 1725." Such an inscription is extremely rare among accomplished Virginia portraits of the period, except for deliberate copies made about the middle of the century by Hesselius and Wollaston. Because its stylistic links to the Bridges group are self-evident

---

[48] John Bolling, Jr. (1700–1757) married Elizabeth Blair (1709–1766) in 1728. Foote, "Charles Bridges," pp. 32–33.

[49] E. G. Swem, ed., *Brothers of the Spade: Correspondence of Peter Collinson, of London, and of John Custis, of Williamsburg, Virginia, 1734–1746* (Barre, Mass., 1957), p. 14.

FIGURE 38. *Elizabeth Blair Bolling*, by Charles Bridges.

FIGURE 39. Detail of Fig. 38.

FIGURE 40. *John Custis IV*, by Charles Bridges.

and because it is the only painting discussed here to bear such an inscription, it is suggested that the Custis portrait is a copy by Bridges of a portrait painted at least ten years earlier. The artist took good care to note the age of the sitter and the earlier date, as seems to have been the practice.[50]

Confusion has also surrounded two portraits said to be of Robert "King" Carter, the powerful landholder and founder of a Virginia dynasty. Carter had died in 1732, three years before Bridges's arrival in Virginia, having written his will in 1726 and included in it mention of two portraits of himself; a subsequent portrait was apparently painted in 1727. A portrait at Shirley, the home of his son John, who had married Elizabeth Hill of Shirley, has long been thought to be of "King" Carter (Fig. 41). On the basis of its similarity to the Shirley portrait, another portrait discovered in recent years has also been called "King" Carter (Fig. 43).[51]

Although the situation is clouded by considerations of tradition and

---

[50] Was it, in fact, a copy of one of the Brodnax–Jaquelin–Ambler group, which are in no sense accomplished but which are frequently inscribed on the front with the age of the sitter? After all, a portrait long held to represent the daughter of John Custis IV, Frances Parke Custis, is included in this group, which remains unconvincingly analyzed, despite Mary C. Black, "Pieter Vanderlyn and Other Limners of the Upper Hudson," in Ian M. G. Quimby, ed., *American Painting to 1776: A Reappraisal*, Winterthur Conference Report 1971 (Charlottesville, Va., 1971), pp. 217–249. See also n. 8 and Richard K. Doud, "The Fitzhugh Portraits by John Hesselius," *Virginia Magazine of History and Biography*, LXXV (April 1967), pp. 159–173.

[51] See n. 8. In his will, "King" Carter (b. 1663) directed that a portrait of himself and his first wife be left to their only son, John. "Carter Papers," *Virginia Magazine of History and Biography*, V (April 1898), pp. 408–428, VI (July 1898), pp. 1–22. He left another portrait of himself and one of his second wife, Elizabeth Landon Willis, whom he married in 1701, to their eldest son Robert. It is likely that both sets of portraits were pairs; therefore, the first pair was probably painted prior to 1699, when Carter's first wife died. It is also likely that the male portrait of this pair is the one that shows "King" Carter as a young man. This portrait has been copied many times and the whereabouts of the original is unknown; it shows Carter, in a blue coat and a long wig, leaning on a table, his left hand on his hip, in a typical Lely pose. For a copy, see Glenn, *Some Colonial Mansions*, I, p. 226. Although it is simpler to assume that the Shirley portraits, long called "King" Carter and his first wife (Figs. 41 and 47), are indeed the same ones that were left to John and Elizabeth Hill Carter of Shirley, my attribution of them here obviously runs counter to that thesis.

FIGURE 41. "Robert 'King' Carter," by unknown artist.

FIGURE 42. Detail of Fig. 41.

condition, a careful examination of these two portraits and the sur-
viving evidence suggests that the recently discovered portrait was
painted by Bridges but is not of "King" Carter, while the Shirley
portrait may well be the work of another painter. In appearance the
latter portrait is quite flat, especially in the face (Fig. 42). Even if this
has been accentuated by what seems to have been fire damage (discovered during a recent cleaning) or by an old, overzealous restoration, it appears that the painter employed mannerisms in constructing
the face that are somewhat different from the ones we have seen
above, although it must be noted that the nature of the brushwork is
similar.[52] Taking the factor of its condition into account, the face of
the Shirley portrait seems to be articulated less capably than the other
male portraits here, the parts less convincingly related to each other
in space. Nor is this an isolated phenomenon, for the same charac-
teristics can be observed, to an even greater degree, in another portrait thought to be a member of the Carter family and previously
attributed to Bridges, the so-called "Charles Carter of Cleve" (Figs.
44 and 45).[53]

This portrait has also been seriously damaged, since it was folded
and buried during the Civil War, but enough remains to suggest the
same features and lack of clear articulation in the face, different, it
seems to me, from other abraded portraits such as *Alexander Spotswood* and *James Blair* (Figs. 18 and 15). Furthermore, the "Charles
Carter" and the Shirley portraits have the same strange, rubbery

[52] The portrait was restored in the late 1960s by Charles H. Olin, formerly chief
conservator, National Portrait Gallery, Washington, D. C. It was suspected at that
time that the unusual surface conditions, particularly noticeable on the upper sides of the
figure, may have been due to heat damage. The theory has been advanced that the portrait
is indeed an earlier one of "King" Carter, which was damaged in a recorded fire at
Corotoman in 1729 and was repainted by Bridges during his stay in Virginia. It seems
unlikely to me that Bridges would have changed the placement of the arms—which shows
so clearly—of an earlier composition.

[53] Charles Carter (1707–1764) was the third son of "King" Carter. Foote, "Charles
Bridges," pp. 33–35. See also Lucille McWane Watson, "The Colonel and his Lady come
home: A case history in the study of colonial Virginia portraiture," *Antiques*, LXXIV
(November 1958), pp. 436–438.

hands, distinct from the more solid and realistic ones that Bridges usually depicted. Yet the condition factor must still be admitted to be a troublesome one. If, on the basis of the visual evidence, these two similar portraits seem to be by a painter other than Bridges ("Charles Carter" especially so), the slender possibility remains that the Shirley portrait was painted by Bridges and that subsequent damage has distorted his characteristic qualities.

Compositionally, the Shirley portrait was given a slightly exaggerated twist to the body, causing the painter some anatomical problems—the changes in the placement of both cuffs and the distortion of the right shoulder and upper arm are conspicuous. No such difficulties mar the recently discovered subject (Fig. 43), whose ease of bearing strongly resembles that of Mann Page II. Indeed, this portrait manifests a real sense of assurance—the pose is natural and relaxed, especially in the gloved hand resting on the cane, the rendition of the gray woolen coat not overemphasized by many highlights, and the strong and well-preserved head providing a satisfactory focus for the composition.

To emphasize further the differences between the two so-called "King" Carter portraits, it should be noted that the original canvas of the recently discovered portrait (Fig. 43) was inscribed on the back in a nineteenth-century hand, "Sir John Howell London 1680," with the name "Dr. W. H. Seldon Warwick Va." The Seldon family had inherited the portrait from the Lightfoot family of Sandy Point, Charles City County, who had intermarried with the Howell family in the mid-eighteenth century. The portrait is described in a late nineteenth-century letter as being among other Lightfoot and Howell family pictures and plate "at Sandy Point or Tedington."[54] Thus it is more probable that it represents a member of the Howell

[54] "Lightfoot family," William and Mary Quarterly, 1st Ser., III (October 1894), pp. 104-111. I would like to thank Mrs. Mary R. M. Goodwin for this reference. The post office at Sandy Point was named Tedington, which accounts for what might seem some imprecision in this description.

FIGURE 43. "Robert 'King' Carter," by Charles Bridges.

FIGURE 44. "Charles Carter of Cleve," by unknown artist.

FIGURE 45. Detail of Fig. 44.

or Lightfoot families than it does "King" Carter, whose relationship to these two families is obscure.

In the same category as the above picture, in terms of solid assurance and convincing physical presence, can be included a well-preserved portrait with some record of a Virginia provenance, known simply as a "Colonial Gentleman" (Fig. 46).[55]

Accompanying the Shirley portait of " 'King' Carter" is a portrait of a woman called "Judith Armistead Carter," the first wife of "King" Carter, who had died in 1699 (Fig. 47). Close comparison with the portraits of Mrs. Mann Page II, Elizabeth Blair Bolling, and the Moore girl (Figs. 4, 38, and 35), especially in the face, points to a convincing Bridges attribution for this portrait, which then leaves the identity of the sitter open to question.[56] Her dress has been given a bravura treatment and could have been intended to complement the effect of the " 'King' Carter" portrait (Fig. 41). Certainly the dark, rich quality of her dress material calls for strong highlights, yet, if the effect created is almost ostentatious, it is still more controlled than that of the male portrait. Such treatment, however, threatens to get out of control in the portrait of "Elizabeth Wormeley Carter" (Fig. 48), which is the most contrived, in terms of English baroque mannerisms, of all the portraits discussed here, even the tilt of the head (observed before in Figs. 4, 7, and 35, for example) being given greater emphasis, the basket of flowers made more abundant, and the ornamental urn in the background more elaborate. Although the subject of this portrait has been called Elizabeth Carter (1683–1719),

[55] Alexander Wilbourne Weddell, *Portraiture in the Virginia Historical Society, with Notes on the Subjects and Artists* (Richmond, Va., 1945), pp. 110–111. The portrait was given to the Virginia Historical Society in 1929 by Herbert L. Pratt of New York City. When acquired by him, it was reputed to have Virginia associations, and was actually thought to be "Governor Johnson of Virginia by Smybert." As there was no Governor Johnson of Virginia, and as Smibert was not then recorded to have been in Virginia (he was, actually, but only for ten days) (*The Notebook of John Smibert* [Boston, 1969], pp. 18, 86), this attribution was considered unlikely. Pratt, however, had reason to believe in some Virginia associations.

[56] Perhaps it represents Elizabeth Hill (d. 1771), who married John Carter (1690–1742) in 1723.

FIGURE 46. "Colonial Gentleman," by Charles Bridges.

FIGURE 47. "Judith Armistead Carter," by Charles Bridges. See color plate facing page 96.

FIGURE 36. *John Bolling, Jr.*, by Charles Bridges.

FIGURE 49. "Augustine Moore," by Charles Bridges.

FIGURE 48. "Elizabeth Wormeley Carter," by Charles Bridges.

it is more likely to be Elizabeth Wormeley (1713–1740), who married Landon Carter in 1732. Since it was painted, the portrait has apparently been at Sabine Hall, Westmoreland County, the house that "King" Carter helped his son Landon build.[57]

Prominent among the final group to be discussed are three other portraits of the Moore family, a pair of three-quarter length in matching original frames called "Augustine Moore" and "Mrs. Augustine Moore and child" (Figs. 49–52), and an appealing Kit-Kat sized one of a young man said to be their son, "Thomas Moore" (Fig. 53).[58] Slender and assured in bearing, "Augustine Moore" stands at his baize-covered desk, with his ledgers and account books kept in an arched-top, recessed bookcase nearby. He fixes the viewer with a piercing look, his head sharply turned, almost at a right angle to his body. His head, in fact, seems especially prominent because of the very thin and flat quality of the painting, with the notable exception of the face, which is more florid and fleshy than any other here attributed to Bridges (Fig. 50). His matronly wife, characterized by Bridges's customary smooth and firmly modeled face and the hint of a smile in her eyes (Fig. 52), supports a rather large child who appears to be seated on a cushion on a ledge, and who bears a definite resemblance to the Ludwell children (Fig. 20), accentuated perhaps by the blue gown of the mother, the red curtain, and the peach. "Thomas Moore" comes forth as an engaging young man, standing in a cocked hat and brown coat with fashionable slashed sleeves and

---

[57] Foote, "Charles Bridges," p. 36. Any reference to the portrait of "Elizabeth Wormeley Carter" must lead to a discussion of the portraits at Shirley called "Elizabeth Hill Carter as a young girl" (Fig. 61), her father, "Edward Hill," and his wife, "Elizabeth Williams Hill." Alexander Wilbourne Weddell, ed., *A Memorial Volume of Virginia Historical Portraiture, 1585–1830* (Richmond, Va., 1930), pp. 109–111. The young girl is a half-length and a virtual duplicate of "Elizabeth Wormeley Carter" in the pose and the treatment of the drapery, the brushwork of which is remarkably similar to Bridges's. Her face and hair are uncharacteristic of Bridges, I am uncertain about this portrait, and much more so about the pair that tradition calls her father and mother, although there are elements about the latter, especially in the drapery, that are similar.

[58] Augustine Moore appears to have died in 1743 (see n. 47); the birthdate of Thomas Moore is unknown.

FIGURE 49. "Augustine Moore," by Charles Bridges. See color plate facing page 81.

FIGURE 50. Detail of Fig. 49.

FIGURE 51. "Mrs. Augustine Moore and child," by Charles Bridges.

FIGURE 52. Detail of Fig. 51.

FIGURE 53. "Thomas Moore," by Charles Bridges.

proudly displaying his fowling piece. The posed twist of the body and head—meant to suggest, perhaps, an informal moment—has already been seen (Fig. 41), and is caught again in the portrait of "Thomas Lee" (Fig. 54), husband of "Hannah Ludwell Lee" (Fig. 19), whose sharp, well-defined features are similar in character to, if somewhat flatter than, those of "Augustine Moore."[59]

Two further Page family portraits, two from the Moore family group, and a Bolling family member conclude this study. "Alice Page" (Fig. 55) and "Mann Page I" (Fig. 56) were both acquired by Dr. R. C. M. Page from the same house in Gloucester County, although many years apart.[60] "Alice Page" strongly resembles "Judith Armistead Carter" (Fig. 47), while "Mann Page I," which is largely overpainted, might well, physiognomically, be a Grymes child (Figs. 28 and 32). Both "Mr. Ainsworth" (Fig. 57) and "Dorothea Dandridge" (Fig. 58) have been so badly worn as to make their attribution uncertain, but a similarity to the other portraits discussed here pervades them.[61] Finally, quite different in her accoutrements but manifesting all the qualities of handling we associate with Bridges is the portrait of *Mary Kennon Bolling* (Figs. 59–60), benign and toothless but with striking large blue eyes and "widow's hood." The style of her dress, particularly the "echelles" bodice, is one that anticipates the portraits we generally associate with the 1750s.[62]

---

[59] Thomas Lee (1690–1750) of Stratford was a burgess and a member, and one-time president, of the Governor's Council.

[60] See also n. 45. Mann Page I was born in 1691 and died in 1730. The portrait was bought by Dr. Page from Mrs. Cornelia Griffith of Shelly, Gloucester County, in 1878. It might conceivably represent one of the three children of Mann Page II (see nn. 23 and 45).

[61] Family tradition states that "Mr. Ainsworth" was an English merchant in contact with the Moore family. There is no way of substantiating this. Dorothea Dandridge (1731–1773), the daughter of Alexander Spotswood, married Nathaniel West Dandridge in 1747. This portrait also descended in the Moore family line, and obviously cannot be of "Dorothea Dandridge" if it is by Bridges.

[62] Mary Kennon Bolling was the wife of John Bolling, Sr. (1676–1729). Her birth and death dates are unknown.

FIGURE 54. "Thomas Lee," by Charles Bridges.

FIGURE 55. "Alice Page," by Charles Bridges.

FIGURE 56. "Mann Page I," by Charles Bridges.

FIGURE 57. "Mr. Ainsworth," by Charles Bridges (?).

FIGURE 58. "Dorothea Dandridge," by Charles Bridges (?).

FIGURE 59. *Mary Kennon Bolling*, by Charles Bridges.

FIGURE 60. Detail of Fig. 59.

Figure 61. "Elizabeth Hill Carter," by unknown artist.

FIGURE 47. "Judith Armistead Carter," by Charles Bridges.

FIGURE 64. *George Booth*, by William Dering.

Bridges's activity in Virginia came at a time when the leading colonists were making a conscious effort to put the seal of sophistication on their successful experiments at settlement in the New World. After a century here society could be considered mature enough to warrant the visible mark of a leisured, or at least cultured, class, with all its attendant flourishes of elegant buildings, fine clothes and manners, and portraits and plate. Westover and Rosewell, for example, two of the most lavish country houses in the colonies, were being completed in the 1730s. Also to be noted is the increase in the survival of written records of this period, which is surely another aspect of the same conscious determination on the colonists' part. It cannot be mere coincidence that two trained academic portrait painters arrived in two of the main areas of settlement in this period, within a few years of each other, and made their own distinct contributions to the visual record.

If Bridges was as active painting portraits in the populous rural society of Virginia as Smibert was in his urban environment, he would probably have completed more than one hundred and fifty during his stay in the colonies, an average of seventeen or eighteen a year. Less than a quarter of that number appear to have survived, the consequence not only of a basically deleterious climate but also of the physical and economic ravages of wars. Those that have survived produce a clear image of the Virginia gentleman and his family that perfectly matches the word pictures evoked by leading historians of this society.[63] The best of these portraits—in the context of provincial painting—convey an unmistakable sense of individual presence and identity, of a distinct posture and preference. That Bridges was able to satisfy the differing requirements of William Byrd II, who owned the nearest equivalent in the colonies at the time to an English

---

[63] See, for example, one of the most recent studies, Edmund S. Morgan, *American Slavery, American Freedom: The Ordeal of Colonial Virginia* (New York, 1975).

nobleman's gallery of pictures, and Commissary James Blair, who seems to have prescribed an uncommon intellectual programme for his portrait, as well as create such convincing and satisfying portraits as *Mann Page II*, *John Bolling, Jr.*, and "Girl of the Ludwell family" was no small accomplishment.

William Dering

Y an unusual coincidence, William Dering's name first appears in the colonial records within a month of that of Charles Bridges. Dering was in Philadelphia at the time and seems to have been, to some degree, already established:

> Mr. Dering, Dancing-Master, gives this Publick Notice that he has now divided his School the Following Manner, viz. On Mondays, Wednesdays and Fridays he teaches the more advanc'd Scholars, and on Tuesdays, Thursdays and Saturdays the young Ones: Every Friday Fortnight will be a publick Night, when the whole School will be together, and all Gentlemen and Ladies, desirous to see their Children or Friends dance, are welcome to come to the School. . . .[64]

More information about his activities appeared in an advertisement almost a year later in the same newspaper:

> At the House of William Dering in Mulberry-Street, is taught Reading, Writing, Dancing, Plain Work, Marking, Embroidery, and several other Works: Where likewise young Ladies and Gentlemen may be instructed in the French.[65]

Dering apparently moved to the Williamsburg area a month or so before Bridges moved away to Hanover County. He advertised in the *Virginia Gazette*, November 25, 1737:

> This is to give Notice, that this Day the Subscriber has opened his School at the College, where all Gentlemens Sons may be taught

---

[64] *Pennsylvania Gazette* (Philadelphia), April 10, 1735.
[65] Ibid., February 11, 1736.

Dancing, according to the newest French Manner, on Fridays and
Saturdays once in Three Weeks, by
William Dering, Dancing-Master

Dering did not take up residence in Williamsburg immediately, however, since a debt suit entered in the York County court in 1739
described him as "Wm. Dering otherwise called J. Wm. Dering of
the County of Glosr [Gloucester]." In August 1742 he bought from
Mr. and Mrs. Henry Cary II two lots in Williamsburg, on which
stood a house now called the Brush-Everard House, a Colonial Williamsburg exhibition building. By this time, to judge from William
Byrd's diary, Dering had met and been accepted by a number of
prominent planters. He was mentioned several times in Byrd's diary
for the years 1740–1741, moving confidently among the tidewater
gentry, supervising (presumably) "Dance day" at Mr. Cary's (June
16, 1741), playing the French horn, arriving from Shirley plantation,
accompanying Mr. Walthoe, and so on. On July 31, 1741, Byrd
specifically noted that he showed Dering his prints.[66]

Dering's career as a dancing master continued through 1747. Described in a legal document of 1744 as "Of the City of Wmsburgh
Dancing Master," he advertised balls and assemblies at the Capitol
in March and October 1745 and September 1746. On May 1, 1747,
the Council ordered Dering to be paid "the further Sum of £20
acct. of an Entertainmt made by him."[67] Yet he seems to have led a
continuously precarious existence financially, being plagued with
debt suits during the period. He mortgaged the lots he had bought,
together with his slaves and household furnishings, to Bernard Moore
and Peter Hay, a mortgage that was assumed by Philip Lightfoot in
1745 and subsequently by his heir, William Lightfoot, in 1749. By
December 1749 Dering had sought greener pastures and moved to

---

[66] Maude H. Woodfin, ed., Marion Tinling, trans., *Another Secret Diary of William
Byrd of Westover, 1739-1741* (Richmond, Va., 1942), passim.
[67] H. R. McIlwaine et al., eds., *Executive Journals of the Council of Colonial Virginia*
(Richmond, Va., 1925-1966), V, p. 235.

Charleston, South Carolina, where, in partnership with one Scanlan, he advertised a ball on December 18. He was still in Charleston in May 1751, having presumably left his wife to face the music in Williamsburg; John Blair noted in his diary for February 14, 1751, that he had attended "Mrs. Dering's outcry" [auction]. Nothing is subsequently known of him.[68]

Listed among Dering's possessions in the mortgage schedule of May 1744 were "8 pictures in Guilt frames 9 Do. in black frames 10 Do. without frames." When the mortgage was transferred in May 1745, his possessions were enumerated again and included "44 pictures some gold some bla[ck] Frames," as well as "1 large hair Trunk with about 200 prints 1 paint box."[69] It is not unreasonable to surmise that Dering had acquired these important items from the departing painter Charles Bridges, and that he saw in them an opportunity to buttress his tottering finances by taking further advantage of his circle of acquaintances—among whom were counted precisely those members of society who could afford to buy portraits.

With due consideration for posterity, Dering unequivocally signed one of his paintings. This is the portrait long regarded as *Mrs. Drury Stith* (Fig. 62). It is inscribed "Ætatis Suae 50" at lower left, and "W. Dering" at lower right. Placed behind an oval spandrel in a typical Bridges pose, Mrs. Stith faces diagonally to her left with the light coming from the upper right. A white shift shows below the bluish gray dress at bosom and forearm, and a robe swirls around her middle to complement the oval shape of the composition. Time and

[68] *South Carolina Gazette* (Charleston), December 11, 1749; Colonial Office, Virginia, Original Correspondence, Secretary of State, 1746-1753, C.O. 5/1338f., 998–1000, Public Record Office, microfilm, Colonial Williamsburg; "Diary of John Blair," *William and Mary Quarterly*, 1st Ser., VII (January 1899), p. 136. Did Dering continue painting portraits in Charleston? A portrait of "Mrs. Anthony Van Schaick" in Margaret Simons Middleton, *Henrietta Johnston of Charles Town, South Carolina, America's First Pastellist* (Columbia, S. C., 1966), illustrated on p. 67, bears an uncanny resemblance to his Virginia portraits, to judge by the photograph, although it has a confusing provenance. It does not seem characteristic of Johnston's work. I would like to thank Molly Prince for bringing this to my attention.
[69] York County Records, Deeds, 5 (1741-1754), pp. 102-105, 136-139.

FIGURE 62. *Mrs. Drury Stith*, by William Dering.

restoration, however, have not been kind to the painting, and it is difficult to consider it particularly appealing now.[70]

Mrs. Drury Stith, the former Elizabeth Buckner, to judge by the known dates of her children, was married about 1717 and thus was born 1695–1700. Given the fact that her age is inscribed on the portrait, it is unlikely that it was painted prior to 1745, presuming that the identity of the subject is correct (the provenance is plausible). As Mrs. Stith was the daughter and wife of burgesses and was born in York County, there was every opportunity for Dering to have known her.

In addition to the signed portrait, there is one further documentary reference to Dering's newfound occupation. The ledger of John Mercer, merchant of Stafford County, contains an account with William Dering for the years 1749–1750. Mercer lodged with Dering while he attended the general court sessions in Williamsburg from 1748 to 1750, and in May 1749 supplied him "sundry Paints cost 29/10 sterl 80 pr ct adve £2.13.9," with which Dering obliged "By drawing my Picture" at the cost to Mercer of £9.2.0.[71]

Closely related stylistically to Mrs. Stith are two recently discovered three-quarter length portraits of a more engaging nature—the young boy especially so. Having descended until recent times in the Booth and Taliaferro families, the portraits have always been known as *Mrs. Mordecai Booth* of Gloucester County (Fig. 63), and her son *George Booth* (Figs. 64–66). As noted earlier, Dering had apparently lived in Gloucester County upon his arrival in Virginia, and one of

[70] J. Hall Pleasants, "William Dering, A Mid-Eighteenth Century Williamsburg Portrait Painter," *Virginia Magazine of History and Biography*, LX (January 1952), pp. 56–63. Although there has been some erosion of the inscription, the age of the sitter does appear to be written as 50.

[71] John Mercer Ledger, 1725–50, fol. 100, Bucks County Historical Society, Doylestown, Pennsylvania. See also C. Malcolm Watkins, *The Cultural History of Marlborough, Virginia* (Washington, D. C., 1968), p. 32. Two portraits have been called John Mercer— one in Watkins, ibid., Fig. 3 (present whereabouts unknown), which bears all the marks of John Hesselius, and the other in Helen Hill Miller, "A Portrait of an Irascible Gentleman: John Mercer of Marlborough," *Virginia Cavalcade*, XXVI (autumn 1976), p. 84, which is definitely by John Hesselius.

FIGURE 63. *Mrs. Mordecai Booth*, by William Dering.

FIGURE 64. *George Booth*, by William Dering. See color plate facing page 97.

FIGURE 65. Detail of Fig. 64.

FIGURE 66. Detail of Fig. 64.

the numerous suits for debt brought against him in the York County courts was by "John and Mordi Booth."[72]

While the poses and color schemes of the two figures are closely linked to Bridges, the theatrical quality of their settings betokens a different artistic nature entirely. Dering seems to have used the English mezzotint not as a strict guide but rather as the point of departure. With arresting ease, George Booth stands in what one must presume was a utopian vision of a tidewater plantation garden. In a pose derived from Bridges's "Boys of the Grymes family" (Fig. 32), but yet more elaborate, *George Booth* competes for the viewer's attention not only with the garden ornaments but also with a dramatic vista of a yet unidentified settlement (Gloucester Point?) that may well have started with a Lely view.[73] Long thought to be an early scene of Williamsburg (Fig. 66), and also suggested as a view from the boy's maternal grandfather's estate, Hesse in Gloucester County, the panorama adds a dimension that is lacking in most of Bridges's portraits.[74]

Mrs. Booth's dress is the familiar blue with a white shift and the curtain is red, but the latter is also elaborately fringed and tasseled and cascades down the portrait and over the sophisticated slab-top table that she leans on. The bold, or simplistic, rendition of her drapery—so similar in nature to Mrs. Stith's—heightens the dramatic

[72] York County Records, Orders, Wills, Inventories, 19 (1740–1746), pp. 75, 80. Mordecai Booth was born ca. 1703 and died ca. 1775. Birth and death dates for his wife are not known; his son George died in 1777.

[73] Such a mezzotint as van Somer's *Duchess of Portsmouth* after Lely is a natural candidate. Belknap, *American Colonial Painting*, Fig. 37. Belknap also pointed out the similarity between this and the early Virginia portrait called "Frances Parke Custis" (Fig. 38B), which ties in with the observations I have made in n. 33.

[74] The vista definitely includes water—probably a river—on the far side, and what seems to be a battery with palisades, guns, and a flag. It may have been intended to represent the fort on the York shore of the York River, or the fort on the Gloucester side opposite (Tindall's Point), both of which were of brick. McIlwaine et al., eds., *Executive Journals*, IV, p. 243. However, neither of the otherwise earliest known views of these settlements, ca. 1755, quite corresponds to Dering's view. Olive Bailey, "Two Virginia Towns 1755," *Antiques*, LII (October 1947), pp. 272–274. In 1747, by coincidence, Mordecai Booth and William Lightfoot supplied rope for the Gloucester fort.

effect, as do the swirling patterns on the light scarlet upholstery, the ribboned bodice, yellow with orange highlights, and the great displays of lace-fringed cuff.

Characteristic of these figures are the long oval faces, the slender aquiline noses, the almond shaped eyes, and the precisely delineated mouths (Fig. 65). The dark shadow areas of the face are defined by a deep carmine, while the hair is swept upward from the brow with broad strokes, and the drapery consists of broad areas of flat color and sharp-edged folds.

Two other portraits of one-time Williamsburg residents share the above features, the one called "Mrs. Charles Carter of Cleve" (Figs. 67–69) and the small portrait of *Dr. John de Sequeyra* (Fig. 70). Formerly regarded as the pendant of "Charles Carter of Cleve" by Bridges (Fig. 44), "Mrs. Carter" is not by the same hand and is confidently attributed to Dering. If the identity of the subject is correct, it would be most appropriate, for Anne Byrd married Charles Carter a few months after Dering moved to Williamsburg and for the next five years they owned the house (now known as the Robert Carter House) directly across Palace Green from Dering's. The artist's propensity for elaborate settings is again indulged, with a rare contemporary view of a tidewater office, fence, and garden (Fig. 69). In the broad sketchy quality of the drapery and the precisely painted face one observes Dering's hand.[75]

Dr. John de Sequeyra (1712–1795) arrived in Virginia in 1745 and established his medical practice in Williamsburg. Although well known to prominent planters such as Jefferson, who credited him with the introduction of the tomato into Virginia, Carter Burwell of Carter's Grove, and George Washington because he treated the Custis children, little is known of his personality. If the paraphernalia on the ledge in front of the oval porthole are not precisely indicative of a physician, there is no reason to doubt the attribution, and de Sequeyra must have seemed a sufficiently unusual figure in Williams-

---

[75] See nn. 26 and 57.

FIGURE 67. "Mrs. Charles Carter of Cleve," by William Dering.

FIGURE 68. Detail of Fig. 67.

FIGURE 69. Detail of Fig. 67.

FIGURE 70. *Dr. John de Sequeyra*, by William Dering.

burg to warrant such treatment. While it is on a more diminutive scale than the other portraits, it still manifests the same artistic idiosyncrasies.[76]

The portrait of "Maria Byrd Carter," second wife of Landon Carter (Fig. 71), was formerly attributed to Bridges, and a copy of it at Sabine Hall to Dering.[77] To judge by what we have already seen, there is no reason to associate such an uninspired production as the latter with Dering, but there is good reason to associate the "original" with him on the basis of the visual evidence. Directly modeled on a Bridges prototype—the pose, the manner of highlighting the drapery, the pronounced tilt of the head (Fig. 72) are all copies of Bridges's manner—the character of the face, the treatment of the hands, and the method of painting still seem remarkably close to Dering's, given the condition factor. Such dependence by an unsophisticated painter on the established academic portraits of Bridges, which Dering must have seen at Shirley, Westover, and other plantations that he visited, cannot be considered unusual.[78]

William Byrd commented in his diary that Dering had visited him in company with Mr. Walthoe, who became clerk of the General Assembly in 1744. The portrait of "Nathaniel Walthoe" illustrated here (Fig. 73) actually hung at Westover and was bequeathed by

---

[76] Harold B. Gill, Jr., *The Apothecary in Colonial Virginia* (Williamsburg, Va., 1972), pp. 60, 95–96.

[77] Foote, "Charles Bridges," pp. 23–25; Pleasants, "William Dering," p. 63.

[78] The Sabine Hall portrait of "Maria Byrd Carter" is exceedingly primitive and may be a nineteenth-century copy of either the (missing) Bridges or Dering version. In the context of the portrait at the College of William and Mary (Fig. 71) is another Byrd family member, "Jane Byrd Page," given to the college by Dr. R. C. M. Page in 1897. It is so completely overpainted that it is impossible to determine, at this time, who the artist was. The inscription in wash on the back is as follows: "Original portrait of Jane Byrd of/Westover—Daughter of Col. Wm. Byrd by his 2nd/wife Mary Taylor of Kensington and half sister/of the celebrated Evelyn—Born about 1730 and/wife of John Page of Gloucester Co./Va./Painted about 1750 by Bridges/Restored by Lauthier of New York 1878/Purchased by Dr. R.C.M. Page from Mrs/Mary R. Hanson [Polly Page] of the "Rowe"/her residence on James River—1878—she/was formerly of *Willis' Fork*/Hon. Mrs. Wm. C. River [Rives?] Va had this/portrait copied about 1870—[and in pencil] by Meyer of Richmond, Va."

FIGURE 71. "Maria Byrd Carter," by William Dering.

FIGURE 72. Detail of Fig. 71.

FIGURE 73. "Nathaniel Walthoe," by William Dering (?).

Mary Willing Byrd to her son, Charles Willing Byrd. It was later described at Brandon as "Mr. Waltham of Williamsburg. A bust, with his hat on."[79] It shares some of the qualities of Dering's manner with the portraits already discussed, but the attribution is more tentative in this instance than in the others.[80]

Three portraits of members of the Randolph family, which now belong to descendants of the family, conclude this study. A pair of portraits said to be "William Randolph of Tuckahoe" and his wife, "Maria Judith Page" (Figs. 74 and 75), may have been among Dering's first essays in portraiture, if the identity of the sitters is correct, for William Randolph died in 1745 at the age of thirty-three. There seems to be a somewhat tentative quality about them, although it may result as much from the damage, especially in the face, as from the inexperience of the painter.[81] As fresh and engaging in her way as *George Booth*, the young woman (Fig. 76) has been called "Mary Isham Randolph," but must be a member of a subsequent generation.[82] In style, the costume is one we associate with the 1750s, notably with the portraits painted by the young Philadelphian, John Hesselius, who made his first incursion into Virginia society in 1750, as soon as Dering had left for South Carolina. Indeed, one of Hesselius's earliest dated Virginia portraits distinctly resembles this painting by Dering.[83] Perhaps it is the white cap (or "pinner") that gives her the charming informal or ingenuous touch that comes through the discolored varnish and losses of original paint.

---

[79] The description continues: "Left a diamond ring to the second Col. Byrd, upon condition that he would permit his portrait to hang up in the same room with those of the noblemen, with his hat on." See n. 26.

[80] In the same tentative category might be included the portrait known as "Miss Clarke, a governess of the Moore family" that descended in the same family as the previously mentioned Moore portraits (privately owned). It has been amateurishly overpainted, but an old pre-restoration photograph in the files of Colonial Williamsburg shows a face that is very similar to those here attributed to Dering.

[81] Maria Judith Page Randolph was the half-sister of Mann Page II.

[82] Mary Isham Randolph died in 1735 at the age of 76.

[83] Doud, "The Fitzhugh Portraits," pp. 161, 170, Fig. 7.

FIGURE 74. "William Randolph of Tuckahoe," by William Dering.

FIGURE 75. "Maria Judith Page Randolph," by William Dering.

FIGURE 76. "Young lady of the Randolph family," by William Dering.

In light of the pervasive charm of Dering's better portraits, it is sad that we do not know more about him as a person—he proved, one suspects, a lively companion. While he cannot in any circumstances be considered a major colonial painter, his brief career served a purpose for the Virginia gentry between the departure of the aged Bridges and the beginning of Hesselius's periodic visits from Philadelphia. Yet Dering practiced a style that was quickly losing favor. It was Hesselius, as a result of his contact with Feke's work in Philadelphia and, in the mid-1750s, the flaccid Wollaston from London, who ushered in the period of the rococo portrait. To our eyes, however, there may well be more pleasure gained by perusing the portrait of George Booth than by any contemplation of Wollaston's facile likenesses or Hesselius's often-distorted renditions of Virginians. It is mainly as another documented chapter in the history of perhaps the most remarkably documented community in the American colonies —Williamsburg—that Dering's importance lies.

Index

Entries in boldface refer to illustrations